# Kisses *of* Cosmic Consciousness

# *Kisses of Cosmic Consciousness*

Dean C. Gardner

Library of Congress Control Number: 2020912262

PAPERBACK: 978-1-952155-55-0
EBOOK: 978-1-952155-56-7



Ordering Information:

For orders and inquiries, please contact:
1-888-404-1388
www.goldtouchpress.com
book.orders@goldtouchpress.com

Printed in the United States of America

# CONTENTS

Dedicated to my 5 grandchildren.

# SECTION 1

## *With What Matters*

To grasp
The mysteries of life
As cosmic consciousness defines
Time and space
The third eye probes
The unknown
With the deep touch.

Although hidden meaning flourishes as the shadows
Of what matters, becoming there follows the light
Emanating from celestial clocks through a portal
To a one-dimensional reality.

It is from there that mind launches self
Into the domain of the given as an epiphany
Of wonder carries the heart with the rhythm
Of pure music.

While meditating upon things in themselves
Becoming there transcends the dull round
And enters the light of the always, already there.

Then, mind beholds the dance of the phantom.

Then, cosmic consciousness rubs life
Into a presence and the shadows
Of hidden meaning embrace the third eye
With visions of eternity.

So, the calculus of time and space
Reveals the unknown as the mystery of life
And things in themselves picture the drift of Truth.

Then, life smiles with understanding.

The romantic feel
Freidrich presents in
"Above the fog"
Takes the look
Into a domain far beyond
The here and now.

The sky
An ethereal elixir
Poured into what is there
Carries the moment
When time reaches
Into the magic
Of becoming there
As space fills mind
With mystery.

Then
The earth groans

Into knots
Of contemplation
The rise of possibility
In thought.

How
The timeless age
Of the always already there
Thrusts cosmic consciousness
Into things in themselves
Rising from the fog
Drawing visions
Of forevermore.

Upon a precipice
Taking his stand
A man with no shadow
Dressed in black
Looks into the expanse
And the landscape
Rises from the drift.

There is
A hollow
In his presence
Where the unknown
In life dances
With the song of Truth
Beckoning
Times and a half
As he seizes
The passage of destiny.

He has reached
The pinnacle

Of celestial dynasties
Launches a plunge
Into the other
As fog conceals
The dwelling of the living.

Then
The man in black
Soars into a thought
Of the deep touch.

An old man sat
Before forevermore
As one day saw
The end of another.

Trapped
By the passage of time
He surveyed a way
To redeem time past
With the hope
Of gathering peace
As his bones ached
And his mind drifted.

Picking his way
Through moments
He recalled the visitation
Of the deep touch
When faith carried him
Through chaos.

Marking each day
As a triumph
He believed himself
Beyond outliving self
As he saw his life
As an odyssey
With the authentic
Article.

He could not lie to himself.

Then
His mind stirred
With magic
As thoughts took him
Into the mountains
Where the wilderness
Tugged on his heart.

So
He became a free spirit
Far beyond self-deception
And he measured his life
With treasures
Found in becoming there.

Preparing himself
For death
He filled moments
With thanksgiving.

Then
He remembered the painting
The Blue Guitar by Picasso

As a song orchestrated
The foundation of his life.

Onward Christian Soldier.

So
The kisses of cosmic
Consciousness
Awoke the patriot
To becoming there
As a first light
Of thought carried her
Into the unknown.

Approaching the domain
Of what mattered
She brushes away
Self-deception
And throttles toward
Truth.

Then
A rush of wind
Burst through
Hidden meaning
And the patriot motored
Through the reaches
Of time and space.

To live
Beneath the star
Spangled banner

Allowed her
The breath of freedom
As she meditated
On The Word.

Her trance
Allowed her to traverse
The expanse
Following the way
The Truth and the life
As her belief
Fueled the moment
With passion.

How
The anthem
Of Truth trumpeted life
Into her soul
As mind empowered
The muscle of liberty.

Then
Belief restored
The triumph of life
Over oppression
As wickedness perished.

So
Ever approaching the center
Of the universe
Delighted her heart
As she felt
The beauty
Of the purple mountain
Majesty.

So
Becoming there is
Always approaching Truth
Through the third eye
A portal to the beyond.

As cosmic consciousness
Penetrates
The heart of the artist
Vision stirs the mind
With the authentic article
And the phantom. dances
In the looking glass.

Time stands still.

Suspended
In the moment
The artist meditates
Upon a figure sitting
In the shade
Of a fig tree.

There is
A world of want
In this figure's heart
His need
To understand
Driven by the void
Within him.

Without a purpose
Time leaves a spirit
In nothingness
A faint echo of life
Ending in a supplement
Of a supplement.

Then
The phantom. leaps
Into a song
As pure music
Elevates
Phenomenal reality
Onto the threshold
Of the deep touch.

Then
The artist configures
The architecture
Of becoming there
As faith establishes
Purpose.

So
Dasein is a figure
Caged in self-deception
While becoming there
Looks onto eternity
Through the looking glass.

Reaching into the unknown
The artist pulls this figure
Onto the rhythm
Of cosmic consciousness.

So
The crows know life
Through the connection
Between becoming there
And cosmic consciousness.

So
The patriot follows
The flight of crows
Into the authentic
Article
As Truth pictures
The dance of ideas.

It was
In a portal
Through time and space
That becoming there
Configured what mattered
From the substance
Belonging
To phenomenal reality.

Then
The sensation
Of the deep touch
Charged mind
With understanding
As passion gripped heart.

From behind
What was there

The patriot conquered
The darkness
In dasein
And the self-deception
Emanating
From dasein.

How
The crows gathered
The hidden meaning
In the thing-in-itself
That portion of life
Extending
Into forevermore.

Then
Cosmic consciousness
Opened the patriot
To a vertical column of time
As the bite of nothingness
Lost its teeth.

There is
An epiphany
In the heart
Of becoming there
That transcends
The here and now
And the patriot listens
To the song of liberty
From a free spirit.

It is through
The close at hand
That the celestial clocks
Reveal the inevitable
As proximity
Between mind and the other
Surfaces.

It is that
Dasein is possessed
By self-deception
And as moment appears
It falls into delusion
After delusion.

Although dasein
Thinks itself to master
The cosmic clock
It plunges ever deeper
Into nothingness;
Then, despair
Is its destiny
Trapped
By outliving self.

A vertical column
Of time governs
The cosmic clock
An attribute
Of the Unknown God.

It is that
This measure
Is experienced
Through death

And joining
With the no longer.

As becoming there
Progresses
Through the window
Of a two-dimensional
Reality
One experiences
A glimpse
Through the looking glass
Through the third eye.

So
Dasein assumes
It is in control
Of phenomenal reality
While becoming there
Always approaches
What matters
Always pursuing Truth.

Dasein is
Its own god
While becoming there
Believes oneself
Toward The Unknown God.

Dasein exists
In self-deception
While becoming there
Lives toward faith
In the way, the Truth
And the life.

It is not
The most beautiful
Of birds
Not the one
With the most
Melodious song
Not the friendliest
But it is the crow
That pulls on the heart
Articulating freedom
For mankind
With the presence
Of the wilds
Stirring the mind
With wonder.

How
The patriot sees
The meaning
Within the crow's flight
Its call
From the wilderness
Endowing becoming there
With the dignity
Of life itself.

There is
Truth in its ways
That transforms
Time and space
Into the splendor
Of a certain blessed assurance

As the authentic article
Triumphs
Over self-deception.

So
The natives
Have a legend
Of the rainbow crow
The most magnificent
Of birds
And how it brought
Fire to the people.

It was
The rainbow crow
That saw
The very young
And very old natives
Freezing to death
In the winters.

It was
The rainbow crow
That had mercy
On the natives
Stealing fire
From the selfish ogres
On the mountain.

It was
This sacrifice
That destroyed
The beautiful plumage
And beautiful voice
Of the rainbow crow.

So
The patriot respects
The crow and all of life.

Then
The troop landed
Across a cemetery
In silence
As the patriot
Stood his ground
In a stand of trees.

It was
That they measured
The distance
In the here and now
While he dug
A hole in the beyond.

Then
His biological clock
Took his breath
Into a moment
Of hush
As he readied
His muzzle loader.

Time shifted
To being and nothingness
As the war
Of principalities
Marched ever closer.

Filling the air
Blood drifted by.

Suddenly
An array of bullets
Charged the hunt
And the patriot
Looked death
In the eye.

Countless were the graves
Of the forgotten
As he remembered
The wall of sacrifice.

How
The brutality of battle
Rose in a moment
When mind relived
The dead and the dying.

So
It was a troop
Of crows
In a cemetery
That brought back
Times of war.

So
War disfigured
Heart and mind
As the patriot lives
The courage
It takes to endure.

To be
In the center
Of the thing-in-itself
Where substance grooms
Being and time
Becoming there flourishes
As a forest filled
With life.

Leaving the illusions
Of dasein
The artist portrays
A radiant scene
Where the spirit of life, itself
Occupies Truth.

There is
A given to the moment
Testifying to the glory
Of The Unknown God
And the artist
Forms that wonder
In the movement
Of light beyond self.

How
The heart reaches
The becoming of thought
As becoming there
Situates the moment
In a parabola of time.

Then
The celestial clocks
Chime the hour
As an awakening
Stirs a time
When Truth takes mind
Into a wilderness of wonder.

Then
Images appear
That cradle becoming there
As cosmic consciousness
Breathes Truth
Into the soul of the artist.

So
A silence fills the moment
As dasein collides
With what matters
And falls into darkness.

With an unsettled mind
The artist looks back
Knowing the depth
Of folly
And then orchestrates
A forest filled
With the authentic article
A triumph of life.

Searching the perimeter
Of time and space

The artist sees
The beginning of an idea
As his phantom.
Carries his heart
Into the deep.

She
Embraces the moment
With the breath
Of life
And his mind taps
Into cosmic consciousness.

It is
The possibility of a thought
Conveyed
Through the canvas
That wraps Truth
Into a parabola of time
As the close at hand
Reveals the tragic face
Of dasein.

So
Becoming there seizes
The magic
Of a thought
While an image
Fastens
To the substance
Of what matters.

Then
The phantom. takes him
Far into the unknown

And he listens
To the sound of her voice
Calling to him.

There is
The touching of passion
That releases the moment
Into the veins of eternity
And the heart
Follows the rhythm
Of Truth.

Then
There was the tickle
Of love pulling
On the celestial clocks
As destiny moved
The artist
Into the source of ideation.

So
Mind is metaphoric
Whereas brain is
Empirically anatomical.

So
She climaxed
During the rub of eternity
As he pictured his trance.

At the ends of mind
Where a hand reaches out

To touch the always
Already there
The phantom. orchestrates
A song
The message
Defining the line
Between becoming there
And dasein.

It is
The measure
Of time and space
Beyond nothingness
As faint echoes
Carry the authentic
Article
Into becoming there.

Then
Living restores life
And the artist
Opens his third eye
To penetrate
The substance
In things-in-themselves.

Then
The phantom. massages
The moment.

How
Dasein hides
In a looking glass
As the mask
Of self-deception

Cripples mind
And the look
Into what is there
Reveals the face
Of nothingness.

How
Becoming there
Follows the phantom.
Into the authentic article
With a faith far beyond
Possibility
A presence within
A vertical column of time.

It is
The holding of Truth
That separates
Dasein
From becoming there
As the Cosmic Clock
Configures predestination.

So
Dasein knows
No faith
While becoming there
Believes in the way
The Truth and the life.

It is
That faith draws
The line
Between dasein
And becoming there.

Dasein sees
Only the void
While becoming there
Beholds blessed assurance.

It is
That the time piece
Of cosmic consciousness
Moves in a vertical
Column of time
And is known
As the cosmic clock.

There is
Only one cosmic clock
And it is eternal
Governing pre-destination.

It is the clock
Of The Unknown God
And all and everything
From beginnings
To ends
Is of the known.

The celestial clocks
Dwell with a parabola
Of time, revealing
The the concealed
And hidden meaning
Through meditation.

They allow access
To the thing in itself
Leading to a portal
Of time and times
And a half
And are known
Through destiny.

The celestial clocks
Are a transitional stage
Where seeking meaning
Points to The Word
As the means
Of redeeming
Nothingness.

It is
The presence of becoming there.

The biological clock
Is the domain
Of phenomenal reality
And moves
Through linear time.

It is the domain
Of time past, time present
And time future
As configured
In the close at hand.

It is
The starting point
Of the always already there

And the given
For becoming there.

There is
Passion in his bones
That takes the artist
Far beyond reason
And into a mad rush
Of a moment.

It grips his heart
Carrying him
Into a feverish frenzy
Where the design
Of desire
Overpowers his senses.

It is
Her voice
That gives him
A deep touch
But he needs
To leave it all behind
Keeping it
As a memory
In the no longer.

Because she is
His great temptation
He needs to stop
The pursuit
To end their bond.

Then
The artist drifted away
As his mind cleared
And his desire
Faded into echoes.

He kept the memories
Of her look
The passage of her breath
And their bond
Left visions of titillation.

To have tasted
Forbidden love
Is a great temptation
All in itself.

So
There was a time
When she filled him
With wild wonder
But he knew
That time must pass.

Then
He found a way
Out of the madness
As silence grew thick.

Then
He found freedom
In sweet memories.

So
A married woman
Captured his heart

How
He wanted
To be free of her.

A white stallion
On a precipice
With a dark beast
On its back
Fought for life
As the expanse
Spoke destiny
Into becoming there.

It was
A hungry bear cat
Thirsting for blood
And hungry for horse flesh.

How
The attack was
Swift and harsh
And the stallion
Battled with the beast
With its life
Weighing in the balance.

In the moment
Drama dominated

As the sky looked on
With threatening darkness.

Straining with fury
The satalli0on reared
Snapping at the beast.

It all was
A time suspended
In terror
The very moment
When the bear cat
Leaped
Upon the white stallion.

It was
A parabola of time
With no other reality
When hunger filled the beast
As the space
Exuded darkness
And the stallion
Responded with fright.

To fight for life
After a life of liberty
How
The passion
Of the moment connects
The here and now
To fathomless terror.

So
The artist
Portrays an attack

On life
As the celestial clocks
Strike destiny
For the phantom..

Then
The other felt the presence
Of The Unknown God.

When a moment begins
For the artist
The linear is set aside
And becoming there
Spear heads a vision.

It is
A time and space
With cosmic consciousness
As the phantom. stirs the inside
Of the close at hand
And the substance
Of what is there
Writes across the soul.

It is
A prayer spoken
From the heart
That brings focus
To the third eye.

When the image ripens
Colors take the form

Of a dance
Into forevermore
With the taste
Of becoming there.

So
Mind attaches hidden meaning
To the mask
Of times and a half
And the artist layers Truth
Into what he sees
In his trance.

As the dawn of ideation
Spreads light
Across the here and now
The phantom. dances
Upon the palm
At the end of mind
And the artist sweats
Magic into the depiction
Of the unknown.

How
The moment reaches
Into the light
Of the given
Portraying the flesh
And blood of what matters.

Then
The music of the always
Already there
Heightens the moment
With the passion of Truth

And the phantom. infuses
The breath of life
Into becoming there.


Here
In the mountain ridges
Of Tennessee
The patriot
Fathoms the deep
Of being and nothingness
A war raging inside
Of dasein.

At one time
He was of dasein
Until cosmic consciousness
Took him into believing
The Word
As he rose
Into becoming there.

How
The awakening
Trumpeted
Through his person
As the patriot
Witnessed
The transformation
Of his heart and soul
Although his mind
Probed the unknown.

It was
Faith that brought
His vision into the matter
Of things-in-themselves
As he walked
Through the wilderness
Guided by
The Unknown God.

Then
The void haunted him
No longer.

Then
He was equipped
To fight outliving self.

So
He learned why
There is being
Rather than nothingness.

So
It was a dawn
Of Truth
That brought him
Into the splendor
Of the everlasting
As the given spoke
Peace into his heart.

Then
The hidden meaning
Of what was there
In the mountain wilderness

Opened him
To another reality
One that touched him
With the way
The Truth and the life.

In a moment
Of deep power
A vision
Turns a raging sea
Into an encompassing
While the beacon
Of a light house shines
As an emblem
Of deliverance.

It is
A sound
Roaring from the depths
And frothing on the rocky shore.

All the ships
Of time past hug
The bottom of the deep
Crashed to pieces
And sunk to a watery grave.

The angry emerald sea
Pounding
The umber crags
Of shore gestures
Toward the unrelenting fury

Of nature
As the crystal surf
Reaches into becoming there.

It is
The gun metal sky
That explodes
The tumultuous frenzy
Although the sea
Dominates the trance.

Slightly off-center
A small island creases
The horizon
And on it a light house stands
Its beacon
Reaching out hope to the heart.

So
This beacon shines
As a testament
Ever watching
In its stand.

So it is
That a great squall
Pounded a small boat
The apostles
Fearing for their lives
While in the stern
The only begotten Son
Of God slept.

With fits of terror
The apostles

Woke Him
And He stood up
Rebuking the storm.

So
Even
The raging sea
Is under His authority.

On this side
Of the window
The other wanders

Undressing
The moment
Naked despair

So
The patriot fought
For liberty
A freedom fighter
Facing death
With courage.

Being thrown into battle
She stood her ground

With tenacity
In the face of tyranny.

The blood of the patriot
Ran through the age
Covering the earth
With the human rights
Of the living.

How
She served lady liberty
Her life destined
For the heat of battle
And victory.

Then
In a moment
She was hit
And hit hard
And her buddies
Carried her to refuge.

They are
Of one mind, one heart
And one spirit
Facing the enemy
With the will to be
As they dedicate their life
To the living.

How
True are these patriots
Who carry the banner
Of stars and stripes

As the land
Of the free and the brave
Fights oppression.

In her scars
She bares Truth
Her life a testament
To becoming there.

How
The prowess
Of her substance
Conquers her affliction
So
Liberty may be
The destiny
Of life forevermore.

It was
With the phantom.
That the artist penetrated
The unknown
Through a portal
In a parabola of time
That allowed him visions
Of being and nothingness.

How
She danced magic
Into his heart
As the authentic
Article surrounded

The artist
With the light
Of hope.

Then
His phantom.
Placed him at the center
Of understanding
And he gathered
The blooms
Of the given.

It was
A harvest of souls
That fulfilled
Times and a half
As The Word
Spoke the way through life
And the phantom.
Drew the image
Of the everlasting
From the breath
Of becoming there.

Then
A crow called
Destiny to take
The artist
Into the music
Of the everlasting
And there
He beheld the promise
Of The Unknown God.

So
Calling onto self
By The Word
The artist answered
The deep touch
Of Truth
And he pictured
The triumph
Of what mattered most
Over the oppression
Of nothingness
And self-deception.

# SECTION 2

## The Rise of the Everlasting

Off in the corner
Of the always already there
A pond of water lilies
By Monet births peace.

It is
Leaving dasein
And all its deception
That triggers
A leap of faith
Into becoming there.

So
The two-dimensional
Reality
Speaks to the heart
As light dances
Across the pond
And the patriot probes
Hidden meaning
For understanding.

Submerged
In the moment
The patriot remembers
The wounds of war
As her scars etch
The moment with pain.

There was
No escape from time past
As the dead shadowed
Her mind
Although the pond knew
No suffering.

It was
The deep touch
Owned by the water lilies
That brought
The redemption of time
And time and a half
As dasein sunk
Into nothingness.

How
The pond reflected
The face of heroes
All those leaving traces
In the here and now.

Then
She felt the rhythm of life.

Then
She beheld hope
In the stars and stripes.

Then
Outliving self faded away.

It was
The hunt
And the patriot
Armed with a crossbow
Surveyed the perimeter.

He was after a white tail
In the mountains of Tennessee.

They were not
As large
As the ones up north
But they were
Good eating
And made good sausage.

So
Dawn struck the moment
And the crows
Called to the wilds.

All else was still.

Then
In the quiet of morning
A slight breeze
Rustled the trees
A peaceful rhythm
Of the living.

Time and space
Suspended
In becoming there
Brought a treasure
Of life
As the wilderness
Of Tennessee
Talked to the heart.

There was
The scent of the forest
Surrounding the patriot
With the deep touch
And he knew that this was
What life was all about.

Several furlongs away
A buck approached
As the patriot loaded
His crossbow.

Waiting
For a good shot
He knelt
Ready
To make his mark.

Then
Rumbling through the brush
A razor back charged him.

Startled
The patriot scrambled
Up a tree

As the wild boar
Hungered
For a piece of him.

To hunt
And to be hunted
The way it is
In the wilderness
Of Tennessee.

Because cosmic consciousness
Designs them
From the always already there
The bond
Between artist and phantom.
Thrives in the here and now.

It is
A matter
Of becoming there
With a vision
For destiny
As being
And nothingness
Battle
Truth versus self-deception.

It is
That the phantom.
Issues the deep touch
As the artist hungers
For her
And the third eye

Configures treasures
From predestination.

Then
The spiritual organ
That they hold
Together
Injects Truth
Into their mind
And they reach
Into the unknown
Unearthing
Hidden meaning.

So
The celestial clocks
Transform their destiny
Through a leap of faith
And they fill their cup
To overflowing
From the sea
Of a parabola of time.

Then
They enter
A looking glass
To grasp
Their becoming there
Through the light
Of a vertical column
Of time.

So
They are one substance.

As time and times
And a half bring
The moment
Into the encompassing
The third eye pictures
The beyond
Through the trance.

So
Passion drives
The center of mind
In becoming there
Far into things
In themselves
To reveal hidden meaning
Within the substance
Of phenomenal reality.

It is
That the trance
Allows a leap of faith
Into the unknown
While the third eye
Sees through the darkness
Of nothingness.

Equipped
With the authentic article
The patriot
Climbs out of herself
And into the given
Where ideas are born.

Then
She seizes the peace
Beyond understanding
As the celestial clocks
Unwind her destiny
And she places her trust
In The Unknown God.

How
The patriot meditates
Upon The Word
To gather Truth
As the power
Of cosmic consciousness
Eclipses being and time.

There is
A treasure
In becoming there
That liberates the patriot
As she reflects
In the looking glass.

So
The Counselor guides her
Through the other
As the blood of freedom
Preserves and protects.

So
Truth soars in the vision
Gained
From a leap of faith.

In a time
Filled with hatred
The patriot wondered
Why the world
Could not live
And let live.

It was
That wars and rumors
Of wars
Punctuated the planet.

It was
That storms wrought
Death and destruction
Across the dull round.

It was
That words got twisted
And deception ruled
The here and now.

Although fear governed
The world
The patriot took
Her stand
On the side of liberty.

It was
A time devoid of Truth.

Although the patriot
Fought on the side
Of the free and brave
Because it was a land
Of hope
This land of promise
Writhed with division
As she bled her destiny
Into the earth.

So
The workings
Of being and time
Corrupted the minds
Until nothingness
Prevailed.

So
The message
Of being and nothingness
Killed hope
Yet
The patriot conquered
Despair.

So
The patriot sought
The peace beyond
Understanding.

Reaching
Toward the beyond

The artist pulled
From the deep touch
At the ends of mind
To deliver Truth.

It is
A moment
That transcends
The dull round
As he liberates
The substance
In hidden meaning.

Among the treasures
Given to becoming there
Thoughts ignite
A passage way
Through phenomenal
Reality
Onto the unknown.

Then
The third eye
Opens time and space
To an image
Radiant in wonder
And the artist steps
Into a parabola of time.

So
A two-dimensional reality
Pictures Truth
Taking the other
Into regions
Beyond the here and now

As the artist
Breathes meaning
Into what is there.

It all has to do
With linear time
Suspended
In the moment
As the secrets
Buried in the now
Dance in the mirror
Of the thing-in-itself.

Then
The mask of dasein
Dissolves into despair
As becoming there
Fathoms
The interstices
Of what matters
Conquering
Outliving self.

So
Truth lives in the flesh
Dwelling
In the always
Already there.

To commune
With the rising sun

The artist went
To the river to fish.

An armada of crows
Sailed above
As the moment spoke
Freedom
Across the purple
Mountain majesty.

Then
The wind swept
Linear time away
As the phantom. basked
In the call of the wilds.

It was
The intoxicating
Fragrance
Of the wilderness
That charged them
With the passion of life
And they felt their heart
Fill with what mattered.

Bleeding across the sky
The sunrise liberated
Mind from all constraint
As cosmic consciousness
Surrounded becoming there
With the breath
Known to the living.

Leaving
The illusions

Of dasein
They threw away
The mask of self-deception
As they ventured
Toward Truth.

There is
A romance in touching
The expanse
As life dances in the heart.

There is
A treasure
In becoming there
When the dawn brings Truth
To mind
As the deep touch
Abounds in the moment.

With a smile
The phantom. looked
At their catch
And she released them
Back to their home
In the river.

To occupy the center
Of time and space
Where ideas pool
In masses
Across the expanse
The phantom. tends

The garden
Of tables and chairs.

The artist
Traveling by his will
Entered that place
With the power
Sourced
From the deep touch.

How
The phantom. embraces
The artist
Where the eternal light
Glows with possibility.

Suddenly
The image projected
By the phantom.
Tickled mind
As becoming there
Grasped
The always already
There.

As the persona
Of ideation
The phantom. pulled
The artist
Into cosmic consciousness
And the dynamic
Of a vertical
Column of time
Took him
Into pure wonder.

Seeing
Through the looking glass
Of phenomenal reality
The artist pictured
The dance of the phantom.
As a radiant figure
As the rhythm
Of the drums
Moved mind into the heart
Of the thing-in-itself.

While the two-dimensional
Reality emanated
From the deep touch
The phantom. connected
The artist
To an understanding
Of the unknown.

Then
In a leap of faith
Becoming there left
The prison of dasein
As trumpets charged
The moment with Truth.

It is
The call of the crow
That takes the heart
Into the rubric
Of the deep touch
As mind unearths

The authentic article
And becoming there
Climbs out of dasein.

There was
A time in the garden
Of tables and chairs
When the here and now
Became the echo
Of life
While the celestial clocks
Stirred visions belonging
To hidden meaning.

To behold
The flight of the crow
Liberates becoming there
From the angst of dasein
As the always
Already there defines
The horizon of destiny.

Then
An armada of crows
Surrounds presence
With the deep touch
Triggering mind
To travel
Far beyond time
And space.

There
In the drift
Of things-in-themselves
Heart sensed the power

Of the authentic article
As self reflected
In a looking glass.

Although
Confronted with nothingness
And buried in despair
Becoming there looked
To The Unknown God
The source of Truth.

So
It is that Truth
Freed dasein from the chains
Of the linear
The birth of becoming there
As dasein sunk
Into the no longer
As the vision of the crows
Entered the given.

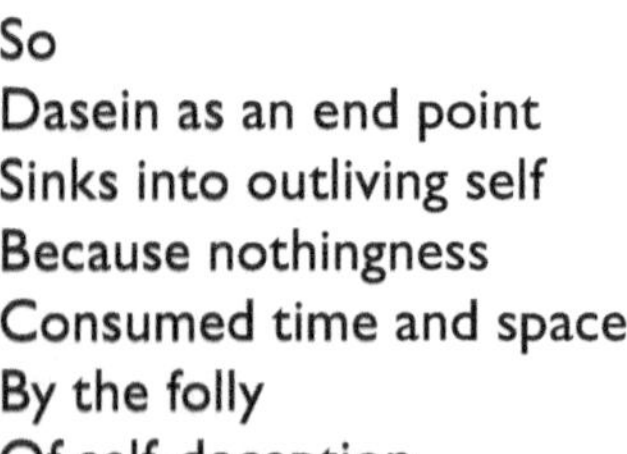

So
Dasein as an end point
Sinks into outliving self
Because nothingness
Consumed time and space
By the folly
Of self-deception.

Thrown into the always
Already there
Becoming there searches

The unknown
For hidden meaning
As possibility dwells
In the light
Of forevermore.

It was
The war between being
And nothingness
The battle
Between principalities
That ripped
The authentic article
Out of the living self
As hope died for dasein.

How
The birth of becoming there
Wills faith
In The Unknown God
As the passion
Of predestination
Enveloped time and space.

Then
The deep touch liberated
The moment
As a two-dimensional
Reality formed
Truth in mind.

To be
With The Word
Became the call of destiny
As becoming there

Unearthed Truth
From the language
Of thought.

Then
Through the deep touch
The Counselor guides
The spirit of the age
Into the everlasting
As dasein
Falls into the pit
Of angst forevermore.

No longer burdened
With doubt
The artist sees Truth
Through the mind
Of becoming there
As an image
Rises from a wasteland.

There is
A stand of trees
Charred by fire
Where life lost
Abundance
As the tombstones
Of stubble
Marked the death
Of a forest.

While the artist liberates
Times and a half
From phenomenal reality
It is Truth
That buries dasein
In the ashes
Of time past.

Then
The mechanics
Of time and space
Delivered the rebirth
Of the land
And the woods sprouted green.

So
What has ended begins renewal.

So
Outliving self brought dasein
To the end point
And hope began
In becoming there.

It is
That the forest
Was of the always
Already there
As the wasteland
Signaled the advent
Of the no longer
But
There is no end
Of becoming there
Because faith carries

Life onto forevermore.

What is a wasteland
Summons the will
To endure
As the artist echoes life
And death.
xxx




So
The biological clock
Keeps its own time
As becoming there
Lives within its constraints
And dasein stumbles
Through self-deception.

So
Becoming there celebrates
The moment
While dasein decays
In the shadows
Of outliving self.

There was
The rhythm
Of a true heart
That connected mind
To the beyond
As the substance
Of a two-dimensional
Reality liberated

Hidden meaning
From the unknown.

It was
The artist who viewed
Time and space
As possibility
Through a portal
In the always
Already there.

To see
Through phenomenal
Reality
And grasp the drift
Of the thing-in-itself
How
The artist allows entrance
Into the authentic article.

Then
Cosmic consciousness
Ignites the experiential
With treasures of hope
As mind launches
Into the moment
With the deep touch.

So
Through a window
In time and space
An image emerges
Taking the whole self
Into the glory
Of The Unknown God.

Then
Truth speaks life
Into the moment
When the biological clock
Reaches toward a vertical
Column of time
And becoming there
Receives the gift of faith.

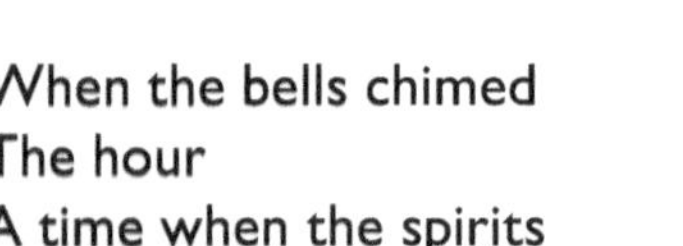

When the bells chimed
The hour
A time when the spirits
Of the dance
Escaped from time and space
The patriot saw
Freedom in the moment.

How
The liberty of her movement
Created images of life
As she seduced
Light from the shadows.

So
The dancer presented herself
As a swirling magic
Filling time with grace
And the patriot
Followed her form
Into an expression
Of the authentic article.

There was
Truth in her body
The way she posed
Beauty in the flow
Of her fluid movement.

Then
The patriot felt
The deep touch
Within the spirit
Of phenomenal reality
As she witnessed
The trigger of her presence
Although he saw her
With the deep touch.

Although
There was distance
Between them
Her dance took his heart
Into epiphany
As the music of the always
Already there
Moved her substance
Into becoming there.

It was
The play of form
A liberation of life
That brought the patriot
Into the center of thought
Where beauty graced
The moment
And becoming there

Felt the awesome power
In the spirit of the dance.

Sitting at the edge
Where nothingness dwells
The patriot slipped
Into this side of Truth.

There was
A stir of pain
As mind passed
Over times past
When flies fed
Upon bodies of death.

How
The kiss of death
Swallowed life
And the heat
Scorched the living.

The blaze of fire
Shot through times
Branding mind
With mutilation.

Then
Memories haunted
The now
As the patriot left
The shadows.

Then
It is tomorrow
That he seeks
Reprieve from the horror.

How
Dreams smash the present
As mind struggles
For the next breath.

The wounds of war
Run deep
And never heal
As the patriot marches
Into death.

It is
In the patriot's eyes
That clouds of poison
Color his destiny
As he continues
In silence.

So
There is a price
For freedom
Paid by those
Who laid down their life
As the living carry on
Wondering
How they endured.

So
Death covers the living moment.

In the garden
Of tables and chairs
The fife visited
Wearing the uniform
Of red and blue
With brass buttons.

It was
His song that moved
The heart
As the patriot marched
Through thick and thin
And times of valor
Signaled the end
Of one war.

It was
Time for the next.

Manet pictured
The fife
As a young lad
Too young to hold
A weapon
But old enough
To wear the uniform
Of war.

It was
A moment framed
By the rhythm
Of courage

With the fife
Carrying the spirit
Of the age.

So
In this garden
Of tables and chairs
The fife tunes
Into the deep touch
And the patriot
Embraces
The rule of Truth.

So
It is a different age
In this here and now
Where the battle
For freedom faces
The oppression of tyrants
As liberty sounds
The rise of the patriot.

How
The savage brutality
In battle leaves traces
In the unmarked graves
As the patriot charges
The ramparts of tyranny
And the fife
Stands his ground
With a song.

Believing himself
Into becoming there
The artist connected
To life
Through the deep touch.

It was
That cosmic consciousness
Allowed mind
To probe the unknown
Through possibility
As the pursuit of Truth
Became his destiny.

How
Hidden meaning mirrored
In the substance
Of what was there
Carried him
Through the expanse.

Following the movement
Flowing
From the celestial clocks
The artist reached
An epiphany.

Then
The garden
Of tables and chairs
Appeared in the darkness
Pictured by van Gogh.

How
The artist knew
The passion of madness.

How
The deep touch
Liberates the mind
From linear time and space
As becoming there
Accepts his predestination.

So
A vertical column of time
Encompasses
All of being
And nothingness
With the vision
That only becoming there
Beholds
As the artist
Composes the dance
Of his destiny.

Then
The blood of time and space
Bleeds Truth into the moment.

Ever deeper into trance
The artist ventured
Far into the unknown
As his spirit willed him
To behold the expanse.

Then
Treasures of thought
Drew pictures in his mind
As a two-dimensional
Reality captured
The thing-in-itself
As a purple flower
Blossomed
In a still life.

To leave
Behind the shadows of dasein
And to leap
Into the vision
Of becoming there
How
Truth speaks to the heart.

There is
The authentic article
In the moment
When beauty
Delivers the deep touch
And mind unearths
Hidden meaning.

To survive the chaos
In a mad world
Becoming there reaches
Into the substance
Of what is there
Pulling on Truth.

Then
His trance

Takes the artist
Into a parabola of time
And the still life
Connects
To cosmic consciousness.

How
The purple flower
Follows the flow
Of Truth
As the secrets
Of the expanse
Open mind
To what matters.

Through the pursuit
Of beauty and Truth
The artist's mission
Climaxes.

Within the walls
Of linear time and space
The constraints
Of dasein
Encompassed each moment
Inhibiting the quest
For Truth.

It was
That the linear
Squelched dasein
As outliving self

Caged the mind
As the lack of faith
Crushed the spirit.

Living in self-deception
Dasein wore a mask
As if it knew Truth
But all that was there
Were shadows of shadows
Supplements of supplements
An endless
Barrier of nothingness.

So
The illusions of dasein
Buried what mattered.

Then
To meditate
On The Word
Brings becoming there
Onto the threshold
Of Truth
As the living moment
Extends self
Into cosmic consciousness.

The walls of linear
Time and space crumble
As a vertical column
Of time
Takes the spirit
Into the center
Of things-in-themselves
And becoming there

Rises into the brilliance
In eternal light.

So
Heart welcomes
The deep touch
Of The Unknown God
As wandering
Through possibility
Opens to wonder
Beyond time and space.

So
Becoming there feels
The liberty
Of a free spirit
Redeemed from time past.

# SECTION 3

## Onto this Side

In the darkest night
An old man walked
Among the graves
Of the distant past.

Silence
Cracked the moment
With the last breath
Of the dead
As the spirits
From another age
Crawled into mind.

In his hands
The old man held life
As times and a half
Fed the here and now
With the no longer.

Then
He uncovered
The living Truth
Of ages past
And the secrets
In the always already
There took him
Into the beyond.

While the rhythm
Carried by becoming there
Brought Truth
As a testament
Toi the living
The old man measured
The inevitable.

How
The workings
Of The Unknown God
Take life
Through phenomenal reality
Allowing faith to govern
The quick and the dead.

It is
The facing of mortality
That liberates life
With the breath
Of forevermore
While the old man
Opens his heart
To The Word.

Then
He steps into the living
Moment
Where the peace
Beyond understanding
Surrounds him with Truth.

Then
The old man witnesses
From his blessed assurance
Thankful for the gift
Of faith.

Traveling
Through the unknown
Where nothingness covers
The close-at-hand
Becoming there speaks
The language of possibility
As time and space
Dissolve in shadows.

It is
The artist who defines
What is there
In images gathered
From the deep touch.

Portraying the substance
Behind a mask of fire
Becoming there reaches
The another reality

Of being and nothingness
As the war
Of principalities
Bombards the moment.

Beneath the embers
Of chaos
The artist pulls Truth
From a free spirit
Dancing in silence.

She is lovely
In her movement
A rhythm caressing
The unknown
With the language
Of the looking glass.

It is
The dance wedded
To magic
That takes the heart
Into the always already there
As mind decodes
The signature of her form.

So
She sprinkles Truth
From her footsteps
Carrying the substance
Of being and nothingness
Into the movement
Of silence.

Then
She removes her mask
And trumpets awaken
The moment
To man being the metaphor
Of Truth.

Then
Far away from the war
Of principalities
The dancer and the artist
Leap into the pure wonder
Of becoming there.

Ever deeper onto trance
The artist beholds
Through the third eye
And witnesses
An epiphany
The glory
Of the land of the free
And the brave.

How
This land
Allows the splendor
Of cosmic consciousness
To flourish
In the heart
Of becoming there.

Then
The triumph of beauty
Over the wasteland
Of dasein
Trumpets a call
From forevermore
And the artist
Forms the substance
Behind the mask
Of the close at hand.

It is
The thing-in-itself
That occupies the artist
As mind drifts
Across the expanse.

So
The phantom. configures
The reality of the other
And she gives
What is there
The uncovering
Of hidden meaning.

So
It is the structure
Of presence
That the artist beholds
As the heart
Of eternity impassions
The moment
With the blood of life.

It is
The way to Truth
That brings the life
Of the artist
Into the power
Of the mindscape
As the harvest of souls
Proclaims freedom.

Believing self
Into becoming there
With the focus
Of the third eye
His phantom.
The artist transcends
being and nothingness.

It is
Through faith
In The Word
That becoming there
Feels blessed assurance
As destiny
Writes across the soul.

Then
The beauty of the given
Shines through the darkness
And Truth appears
In the third eye.

There was
A time within
The here and now
When mind struggled
As the ache
Of dasein
Brought outliving self.

How
The heart throbbed
With violent surges
As the illusions
Of dasein broke
Mind into shards
Of self-deception.

While in the depth
Of delusion
Dasein came to a time
When cosmic consciousness
Showed self the Truth
And the folly
Of times past
Heaved the soul
Into weeping.

How
For times past
Mind glorified self
As the here and now
Was all that mattered.

Then
An awakening crushed
The dwelling of dasein

And there was
Despair.

Then
Dasein entered
The domain of hope
As faith
In The Unknown God
Eased the pain.

So
The Counselor taught
The inside of self
To breathe in The Word
As becoming there lived
Toward Truth.

As a patriot
Left the linear reality
Of dasein
For the beyond
Cosmic consciousness
Took him
Beyond the wilds
Of the unknown.

There was
A brilliant blue
That set
The realities of the given
And a portal opened
In the expanse.

Leaving the temptations
Abounding
In the here and now
The domain of dasein
He went with Truth
As the close at hand
Revealed things
In themselves.

How
Visions of eternity
Shone with splendor.

How
The moment
Of forevermore
Endows
Becoming there
With a heart
Of freedom.

Then
The patriot
Felt the promise
As The Word
Adopted him as a child
Of The Unknown God.

So
The body and blood
Of deliverance lights
Becoming there
With the peace
Only faith provides.

So
In this life
Hope feeds the soul
With true love
And self grows
With the promise
Of the everlasting.

Then
Time and times
And a half allow
Becoming there
To enter the threshold
Of the cosmic clock
While dasein
Outlives self.

Eternity
At the next step
Brings
An awakening
As the sun moves
Shadows
Into the here and now.

How
The everlasting
Extends
The living moment
And becoming there
Trumps times and a half
With possibility.

Whose image
Hides behind the mask
Of nothingness
When thoughts probe
The unknown?

So
Faith leaps
Into the beyond
Carrying the spirit
Of destiny
Into the third eye
And mind encompasses
What matters.

How
The breath
That takes in
The moment
Liberates
Being and time.

So
The light of passion
Serves the vision
Of hope
As becoming there
Ingests destiny.

There is
A song in the wind
That carries Truth
Into the heart
As time and space

Turn clarity
Into mind.

There is
The taste of immortality
In times of belief
As cosmic consciousness
Feeds the living moment.

So
Becoming there
Bares a smile
Welcoming the beginning
Of what truly matters.

Suggesting night fall
Phenomenal reality
Chooses indigo
For the sky
In a vision entitled
The Workers.

A vast field
Of grain
Bearing soft yellow tones
Stretches
Toward the pitch
Of the horizon
As three souls
Harvest
What they had sown.

Two of the workers
Bend to gather
The grain

While the middle one
Looks
To the artist
And sees the viewer.

So
The artist, the viewer
And one
Of the workers
Share the moment.

So
There is a witness
In the field
Still in space
Where time ceases
And she transcends
What is there
As the other.

In a sense
Two bow
Before the field
Focusing on their labors
While the third
Acknowledges
A standing of awareness
In time and space.

She is
Situated in phenomenal
Reality
With a consciousness
Of becoming there.

Although she is
A worker
She transcends
The moment.

Curious enough
She leaves no shadow.

As it is written:
The harvest is great
But the workers
Are few.

Playing in the garden
A lady and her hat
Tickled by the blooms

Through the window
A blank stare
Shadows moved

It was through
Faith in becoming there
That there was
Such a thing as Truth
That brought
The patriot

Into the domain
Of cosmic consciousness.

Although some believed
That there was no
Such thing as Truth
He knew that all things
Were a possibility
And he knew
That much of life
Belonged to the unknown.

So
He probed the unknown
Ever seeking Truth.

Then
Time and space opened
Phenomenal reality
As The Word touched
The substance
Of becoming there.

It was
That the patriot
Felt Truth stir
His soul
As the encompassing
Pointed the way
To what life was
All about.

It was
That becoming there
Was meant to be

Toward Truth
That knowing Truth dwelled
In something beyond self.

It was
That his time past
Required redemption
He knowing
That he had fallen short
Of what mattered.

Then
He felt the presence
Of The Unknown God
And there the patriot
Found his destiny
As a follower
Of The Word.

Time shifted
To being toward
The glory
Of The Unknown God
Although being wayward
Was part of his blood.

So
Cosmic consciousness
Is the attribute
Omniscience
And that attribute
Belonged
To The Unknown God
Only.

How
The patriot
Learned his need
For deliverance
From his self.

With the sweat
Of muscle in the wind
In the heat
Of a summer's day
According to the celestial clocks
Destiny writes
Across the sky.

Then
The other awakens
From a life in the deep
And desperately looks
To a stand of trees
Where the crows gather.

It is
That life begins
In the deep
And ends
In the deep.

To know
Where one comes from
And where one ends
Shadows the drift

Of things-in-themselves
As the other searches
For reason.

So
The cognition
Of what is beyond
Defines the geometry
Of becoming there
As cosmic consciousness
Surrounds time and space.

Then
A massive chasm
Separates the other
From life
And one turns
To the unknown
Because that is
All there is.

So
The search for reason
And Truth leads
To all directions
As mind spins
Through gyres
Of nothingness.

Trapped in the heat
The other seeks
The secrets of this life
While heart feels
The nearness of the grave.

So
One follows the crows
Across the debris
Of the wasteland
To the rise
Of The Word.

Then
The one is born
Again
As time shifts
To the cosmic clock.

It was his calling
To be an artist
Who depicted Truth
In a world known
As a wasteland.

How
Fragile this place
Cluttered with nothingness
And at the edge
Of destruction.

He wanted
To plant the hope
Of The Word
Where a void populated
The mindscape
As dasein

Spoke turmoil
Into time and space.

So
It was a moment
When thought found
Becoming there
As the promise
Of The Unknown God
After finding
The way to live
Toward Truth.

Then
It was to be
A fisher of men
Taking the heart
To a new life
One that listened
To The Counselor.

Then
Cosmic consciousness
Took mind
Into a vast peace
A place governed
By Truth
And the artist
Pointed to the return
Of The Word.

There was
A music to the moment
That awakened
A valley of dried bones

And the artist portrayed
Truth in life.

So
The artist unmasked
Phenomenal reality
With every brush stroke.

So
To serve
The Unknown God
Filled the artist
With blessed assurance
As well as
The authentic article.

A body of flesh
Exploded
By the rush of passion

To look,
Into the substance
Of phenomenal reality
Launches the trance
Where being and nothingness
Wage the war
Of principalities.

It is
The battlefield

Of thought
Where mind wrestles
With the void
As despair attacks
The will to be.

How
The center
Of what matters
Defines the destination
Of a journey
Into the unknown.

Then
Heart joins the rhythm
Of the given
As the celestial clocks
Count milestone
After milestone
Into possibility.

So
Time and space
Leave the moment
And the trance
Carries mind
Into the light
Within Truth
As life reaches
For the deep touch
Of cosmic consciousness.

At that point
In the moment
Heart feels its way

To the an other reality
Of being and time
As becoming there
Triumphs
Over nothingness.

So
The way through
The abomination
Of what was there
Mind sought
The will
Of The Unknown God.

Then
Off in the horizon
Hope rose
Through the blood
Of The Word.

Focusing on the flight
Of a crow
The artist climbs
Out of his self
To visit
All sides of the unknown.

Leaving time and space
He trances toward Truth
As realities shape
His journey
Into possibility.

So
In the unknown
All things are possible
As mind projects
Into things
In themselves
And the scene
Of becoming there
Liberates heart
From the constraints
Of the biological clock.

It is
Phenomenal reality
That contains
All and everything
Of the close at hand
As opportunity
Allows the leap
Beyond what is there.

Then
The artist pictures
The elements
Of being and time
As the crow takes
Becoming there
Into the vast regions
Of possibility.

How
All and everything
Takes the trance
Into the will
Of Truth

As the artist bleeds life
Into a parabola of time.

So
Following the crow
Takes the artist
Into the domain
Of the authentic article
Where the moment
Shapes substance
Into the form
Of the everlasting.

Then
The artist traces
The moment into life.

It is that
Time and space open
To a corridor
Of things in themselves
Allowing becoming there to touch
Cosmic consciousness.

How
The understanding
Of the other
Unleashes hope
As phenomenal reality
Stands within mind.

To see
The bones of thought
Fortifying the abstract
Behind the skull
Throttles the self
Into possibility
And the grandeur
Of what matters
Occupies
Being and time.

The substance
Of the moment
Within time and space
Rises into mind
So the heart of eternity
Yields cosmic
Consciousness.

Then
In that time
Becoming there
Climbs out of self
Finding the trace
To the heart of eternity.

Then
Life begins
With purpose
As the third eye
Sees the magnitude
Of things in themselves.

How
The mind connects

To the inner parts
Of phenomenal reality
As the other
Embraces the substance
Within becoming there.

So
In time and space
The moment occupies
Possibility
With hope
Transcending
The here and now.

This rendering of Matisse's
Woman With A Hat
Conveys a contrast
Of form and substance.

The brightness
Of the background
Carries through
To the woman's face
And her fan
A parallel of pastels
Vibrant in its radiance
Suggesting
A lighter mood.

There is, however
The heaviness
Of her hat

With the dominance
Of darker tones
As a contrasting
Element.

Within her expression
There is
Her painted face
With bright accents
Contrasted
With the look in her eyes
And the set of her lips.

Although her features
Are vibrant
The sentiment
Of her look appears
As though her dark eyes
Reveal a seriousness
Perhaps a pain
Gripping her heart.

The colors
Of this piece
Show a light heartedness
But it is
Only a mask
Concealing an inner trouble
Weighing on her thoughts.

The massive hat
Weighs heavily
As a trace
To the woman
Behind the mask.

At best
She bares the look
Of concern.

So
Mary and Martha
Are a contrast:
Mary listening to the words
Of the Christ
While Martha
Was ever worried
With the preparations
For the Messiah
And the Apostles..

The Woman With A Hat
Is a persona of Martha.

Spiders in the mind
Hollow
Are the thoughts

Crying before the impossible
Then, the little turtle
Sails in the wind

The dagger
Of thought penetrates
The moment


It is
The interaction
Of the close at hand
And becoming there
That defines
Phenomenal reality
While the beyond
Contains the other
As well as Truth.

So
Dasein is
A raw object
While becoming there
Is the subject
In time and space.

How
The equation
Of being and nothingness
Limits cognition
To the here and now
While the physics
Of the authentic article
Expands what is there
Into trumpets of wonder.

Then
Passage into the unknown
Through the third eye
Allows access
To the things-in-themselves
As trance leaves
Traces to the heartbeat
Of cosmic consciousness.

So
The artist forms
The substance
Of the concealed
While becoming there
Witnesses the architecture
Of Truth.

It is
The reflection of time past
Into time present
That precipitates
Redemption in time future
Because The Word cleanses
The living moment
And all that there was.

To live
In the moment
Of forevermore
How
Becoming there reaches
Toward Truth
And The Unknown God
Takes this life

Into the peace
Beyond understanding.

So
Philosophy begins
Where the close at hand ends
And theology begins
Where philosophy ends.

Meditating on The Word
The artist sees
The beauty in the Truth
Because becoming there
Surrounds the moment.

It is
That the trance
That allows
The penetration
Into the substance
Of what is there
As all of life
Launches the history
Of the deep touch.

Then
The artist draws
The breath
Of a parabola of time
As being and nothingness
Define the universe
Of possibility.

While passing through
The moment
The artist dwells
In the wilderness
Of the beyond
As he seeks
The face behind
The mask of dasein.

So
The moment
Between the artist
And the deep touch
Allows entrance
Into the unknown
And mind
Sketches the concealed.

Then
Truth surfaces
Through the presence
Of The Unknown God.

Then
The artist hears
The call of the crow.

Then
The Counselor opens
The heart
With the deep touch.

So
Belief in the Truth
Defines

The breath of eternity
As the artist lives
In the moment
Beyond time
A suspension
Of the here and now.

So
The deep touch
Allows
The presence of beauty
To be
As the artist forms
The image of possibility.

# SECTION 4

## *The Leading Edge*

So
The sun brought hope
At dawn
And Vashakmadze
Pictured the rolling fields
Of iris blue
The flowers covering
The hills to the horizon.

At that point
The sun radiated
Through the pulse
Of becoming there
And the artist fed
Peace with faith.

It was
The presence of beauty
That made the now
As promise
Of forevermore

As the gift
Of that presence
Rose in the soul.

Written across mind
Was the message
Of eternity
As the internal treasure
To the scene
Moved the will to be
Into the blood
Of what mattered.

So
A figure walked
Through the fields
Carrying the labor
Of destiny
As the moment
Transcended
Phenomenal reality
And the beginning of Truth
Touched the soul.

Then
The scene offered a prayer
Reaching through cosmic
Consciousness
Giving the other
A bounty of Truth.

How
The other saw
The image enter eternity
As one traversed

Time and space
Through a portal
In what was there.

Then
Hope pictured Truth
Into the face
Of becoming there.

So
Truth is the beginning
Of the now.

Then
The rains came
And the patriot
Escaped
From bondage
Into the mask
Of times and a half.

There was
The drop of dasein
In self-deception
That brought
The down pour
When
The world suddenly came
Into the close at hand
Debilitated
By being and nothingness.

So
The patriot
Faced the void
Listening to the wild thunder
As becoming there
Took to the looking glass
Finding a reflection
In the war
Of principalities.

Probing the unknown
Mind sketched a river
The water deep
Into silence.

Beside the still waters
He placed thoughts
Toward the encompassing
As the figure
Of what mattered
Danced in the rain.

How
The moment
Equated time past
To the rumblings
Of what was there
As the war
Ran with blood.

Suddenly
Music
Of the authentic article
stirred the heart
as Truth pictured

the way through
hidden meaning.

There was
Deliverance in this moment
Of becoming there
As the patriot
Believed himself
Into the fortification
Of blessed assurance.

The rain and the river
Were his silent avengers.

Because there was Truth
There is hope
As Truth embodied
The deep touch
Of cosmic consciousness.

Building the apparatus
Of what is there
The artist forms
What occupies the living breath
As the phantom.
Takes his thinking
Into the unknown.

It is
In the reaching
Toward the fulfillment
Of a moment

That the phantom. offers
A destiny
Of becoming there
As heart drives passion
Into time and space.

So
The connection
Between the artist and phantom.
Transforms
The biological clock
Into a parabola of time
The domain
Of the celestial clocks.

So
It is the allowing
Of the deep touch
That infuses the authentic
Article
Into a presence
The persona
Of being and nothingness.

Then
Across nothingness
The movement
Of an anthem carries Truth
Into the heart
Liberating the substance
Of the concealed.

How
The artist dreams
The picture

Behind the mask
Of the other
As a portal
To the beyond
Teaches the living
About life.

To stare
Into the bowels
Of nothingness
To be drained
Into the pit
Of tribulation
How
The earth inside mind
Heaves a final breath
Before entering
The abyss.

With no destination
No purpose
Self faces
Outliving self
As the heart muscle
Atrophies
And the limbs
Dangle
In time and space.

To be
One's decay
As the eyes

See only darkness
And shadows
Of darkness
How
The self shrivels
In despair.

Then
Struggling with the dry bones
Of destiny
Where hope pours
Into a mass
Of mud and sweat
Becoming there reaches
For Truth
A life-long service.

There is
A moment
Before annihilation
That picks up
The spirit
As the last song
Trumpets the no longer
Yet
Life continues
In agony.

So
The journey
Is over
And the here and now
Drops its mask
Of hope.

Then
To believe oneself
Out of turmoil
Becoming there grasps
The full round
Of Truth
As The Word delivers
The peace
Beyond understanding.

It is
The third eye
Allowing a passage
Into faith
That brings purpose
Into life
As becoming there
Witnesses Truth.

As echoes
Of time future
Resonate
With time past
The way
To cosmic consciousness
Births the wonder
Of breathing in
The authentic article.

To sing
In the presence
Of The Unknown God

Fills becoming there
With Truth
And the journey
Through the here and now
Materializes
As service to faith.

Although weak
And weary
Self conquers fear
Fortifying self
With the power
To be.

Although crippled
By time and space
The spirit of being one enters
Cosmic consciousness
Through the third eye
And faith prospers
In The Word.

How
The moment
In time present
Lifts the spirit
Until joy and wonder
Take what one is
To new horizons
And places of peace.

How
The mountains of mind
See the destiny
Of heart

As the soul
Transcends being
And nothingness
The battlefield
Of principalities.

Then
Life purposes becoming there
Through the third eye.

It is
All about the trace
To the substance
Of becoming there
The inner part
Of phenomenal reality
While touched
By cosmic consciousness.

Employing softer colors
That vibrate
In their juxtaposition
Matisse reveals
The essence in his view
Of Landscape at Collioure.

There is
A rhythm in the blue
Of the bay
As the building
In the center
Of the image

Dominates the view
After the masks
Of phenomenal reality
Drop away.

Vivid
In its vibration
The life
Of Collioure
Breathes the movement
Of variations of reds
With the blood red
Of the foreground
Matched
With the magenta
Of the coast
In the background.

As the architecture
Of becoming there
Lights with the warm
Insinuation of the other
There is nothing
Threatening
But rather a welcoming
Of the human spirit.

It is a city lit
With the magic
Of inner dimensions
And a calling of peace
From the very essence
Of what matters.

It is
A city living
Through the beyond
Onto the looking glass
Of cosmic consciousness.

So
When the seventy-two
Were sent out
They stayed
In the welcoming homes
But swept the very dust
Of their shoes
Behind those towns
That rejected them
Leaving no trace
To the wayward.

Feet go
Across the field
Mind stays put

The heart pounds
A drum
To eternity

Angels in the back yard
All of them
Spreading the good news


To face
The second death
Becoming there calls out
For mercy
Because perfection
Is required,

Judgement
Measures an account
Of the living
And self knows
That the past
Was at times wayward.

Facing
Eternal suffering
Brings mind
To Truth
As the heart
Knows the steps
Taken along the way.

There is
No one to blame
Other than self
As the record
Of a life

Finds little reason
For the soul to inherit
Eternal bliss.

So
Guilt weighs heavy
In the heart
And mind finds
No hope.

For a life
Facing final judgement
How
One knows
There is no valid excuse.

How
Can one be
Perfect
Through all the past?

Then
The soul surrenders
Pleading for mercy
And seated on
The mercy seat:
Confession
And humility facing
The final judgement.

So
No one is good
No not one.

So
Forgiveness is given
And the name
Is written
In The Book of Life
Because of faith
And faith alone.

As the clouds
Pass over
The mountain ridges
And time and space
Leave no trace
To the other
Becoming there believes
Self out of oblivion.

There is
A rumbling
Of a moment
That connects
To cosmic consciousness
Bringing mind
Into seeing
Through the third eye.

Then
The clouds clear
And an anthem
Celebrates the heart
That bridges
The chasm

Between being
And nothingness.

So
Becoming there does not
Suffer the second death.

So
Nothingness is the despair
Of outliving self.

How
Faith brings life
Abundantly
Enduring the tribulation
And all
Of time and space
Fill mind
With treasures.

There is
An echo across
The mountains
Taking to cosmic
Consciousness
Liberating the self.

Then
The who
Of what one is
Increases as heat purges mind
Until only faith
Fills the expanse.

So
Hope brings life.

The green
Of the leaves hides
The bones of time past

The dagger
Of thought
Penetrates the moment.

Seeing beyond mind
The third eye
Dissolves phenomenal reality

To fly
With the crows
While the mountain ridges
Speak to the soul
Time and space
Configured the battle
Of principalities
As becoming there bleeds
A tempest of hope.

Struggling
In the wilderness
To gather the things
In themselves
The third eye emerges
Showering the heart
With Truth
As a blaze of fire
And cosmic consciousness
feeds mind with blessings.

There is
A vision of eternity
In the call of the crow
That liberates
The soul
And the insides
Of the other
Reveal the will
That belongs
To celestial time
The substance of destiny.

So
The wilderness
Of the here and now
Takes the soul
Into the domain
Of the promised land
As time
Treasures the moment
When becoming there
Takes to flight.

Then
The will
Belonging to the heart
Mind and soul
Resurrects the flesh
Into the everlasting
And the crow
Finds safe haven.

So
There is no reason
To worry
For The Unknown God
Provides.

Beneath the surface
Of phenomenal reality
The authentic article
Emanates Truth
Although darkness
Surrounds its glow.

How
The will to be
Fortifies the vision
To behold
As the clutter
Of appearances
Distracts
Being and time.

To focus
Upon the moment
When the edge
Of possibility
Takes dreams
Into the heart
How
The works
Inside mind seek
For a vertical
Column of time.

Then
Time and space
Dissolve
Into the brilliant light.

To transform
Hidden meaning
Into the seeing of life
Allows Truth
To enter the domain
Of the here and now.

This moment
Transcends
Time and space
As becoming there
Spirits away
Time and times
And a half.

So
The moment
Touches the soul

With the vision
Of celestial dynasties
And possibility
Traces the footsteps
To Truth.

Then
On the wings of eternity
Becoming there soars
Into the province
Of the authentic article.

So
Truth lives
Through the faith
To be forevermore.

To connect
With cosmic consciousness
The third eye
Allows the elements
Of being and time
To transcend
The here and now
Onto a vertical column
Of time.

In the opening
Of phenomenal reality
Becoming there leaps
Into the unknown

With the promise
Of the everlasting.

How
Leaving linear time
Extends mind
Into a moment
When the presence
Of The Unknown God
Delivers self
As the heart meditates
From alpha to omega
And back again.

It is
The rhythm
Of the dance
At the edge of oblivion
That takes becoming there
Into the spirit
Of a looking glass
And time
Loosens the grip
Of self-deception.

While a vertical column
Of time
Touches the soul
Mind transcends
Into the beyond
Liberating
The face behind the mask
As the perfect light
Of The Word
Works the miracle

Of seeing
Things in themselves.

Then
The self fills
With the treasures
Of the always already there
And The Counselor
Guides the living
Onto what matters
Most.

The oil painting
Entitled NO RETURN
By Vashakmadze
Leaves traces
To a mystery.

It pictures a train
At a depot
But is it coming
Or going?

Is it
A case of arrival
Or departure?

Meeting the horizon
The sun
Is either rising or setting.

Certainly
The snow filled tracks
Contrast
With the emanations
From the sun
A warming take.

It is
Almost as if
The sun yields
A tunnel of light
Promising
Either a beginning
Or end.

Curious enough
The vacant tracks
Lead directly
To the sun.

Spotting
The depot
Figures are portrayed
As some standing still
While some are walking
But are they waiting
For someone
Or are they going
To board the train?
It is a mystery
Spelled out
In the cold
Of a winter's day.

The context
Of the moment
Is unknown.

So
There was a rich man
And a poor one.

The rich man received
His reward
In the here and now.

So
Both died
The rich man
Burning in agony
While the poor one
Was embraced
In Abraham's bosom.

The rich man cried out
To the poor one
To give him water
Because he suffered
The second death
But there was
A vast chasm
Between them
A chasm
That could not
Be traversed.

There was
No return
For the rich man.

In the garden
The daisies
Talk Truth

Beneath the briars
Silence
Moves the violas

Beyond the fence
A train
Traces of civilization

It is
That it was
The always already there
In the reflection
Of the looking glass
That brought the moment
Into a parabola of time.

Then
While meditating
On The Word
A vision of eternity

Allowed hidden meaning
To enter
The close at hand
As becoming there
Probed the quadrants
Of what was there
In search
Of the authentic article.

There were
Spirits in the wilderness
Where the beginning
Of Truth dwelled
And life
Took to the passion
Of what matters.

How
The rhythm of a dance
Released the moment
As time and space
Took to the pounding
Of drums
As the interstices
Of mind formed
The battle
Between being
And nothingness.

Then
Hope trumpeted
In the thoughts
Of becoming there
And the celestial clocks
Touched the soul.

As Truth
Dropped the mask
Of self-deception
A vertical column
Of time drove heart
Through the looking glass
And the substance
Of the other defined
The secrets of the always
Already there.

To live in Truth
Liberates images
Of forevermore
As hidden meaning
Appeared
In The Book of Life.

So
Truth is the beginning
Of becoming there.

Belonging to the visions
Of eternity
The dance surpasses
Time and space
As a graceful form
Liberates the soul.

How
Beauty becomes
The treasure

That carries Truth
Into heart
As pure substance
Triggers an epiphany.

Through the third eye
Mind touches
Cosmic consciousness
As the wonder
Of the authentic article
Endows true art
With faith.

To be
With the spirit
Of Truth
How
The moment explodes
With the grace
Of beauty.

Then
Passion drives heart
Into the immaculate
And becoming there fills life
With the splendor
Of The Unknown God.

There is
The flow of song
Penetrating
The deep of mind
That transcends
The war
Between being and nothingness

As the amazing grace
Of beauty pours
Into the moment.

So
The substance
Of phenomenal reality
Reaches into the bones
Of what matters
Giving life to the living.

How
The dance takes becoming there
Into the reaches
Of hope
As dreams picture
The resurrection of Truth.

As the substance
Of becoming there works
Through time
And space
Cosmic consciousness
Restores the vitality
Of the authentic article
Into the moment.

It is
The hour when accounts
Are weighed
And The Word sees
Through time past

As if it happened
In the now.

Then
Mountains crumble
Into the sea
And the moon turns
Into blood.

How
A life pours
Shadows of Truth
Into the close at hand
While times and a half
Reach into the soul.

So
The masks
Of self-deception
No longer conceal
The transgressions
Of blind want
As a pure heart
And clear mind
Is desired
Before the thrown
Of eternity.

So
All have transgressed
And fall short of the glory
Of The Unknown God.

So
None are good
No not one.

Then
Settled on the mercy seat
Becoming there confesses
Hoping for deliverance
Through The Word.

Then
Faith in The Unknown God
Redeems
A soul forevermore.

Looking for what
The future holds
A Young Girl at a Window
By Rembrandt
Looks for her destiny.

It is with innocent eyes
That she sees a world
Leading her into wonder
But the view is the world
Looking at her.

She is not afraid
But rather
Curiosity fills her
With a calling
As she seeks her place.

So
What will the world
Have with her?

In her dreams
She carries hope
As what is there
Teases her.

With her hand
Held over her heart
She feels her destiny
As the unknown
Takes her
Into the romance
Of being and time.

Innocent
She feels
That the world
Wants her
To have a starlit life
Where she prospers
In the fullness of time
As a chosen one.

How
The world spells her
With treasures
Of thought
As it takes her
Into wonder.

How
The world fills her
With the magic
Of youth.

Hopes and dreams
The world gives her
As she believes herself
Into a destiny
Of times and a half
But it is that the world
Sees her as she is.

As Jesus said
Let the little children
Come onto me
For the kingdom of God
Is made for such as these.



The bones of yesterday
Broken
By the mad red dog



Surprised
The door opened
Nothing there

The wilderness of thought
A tree falls
The birds chuckle

# SECTION 5

## *The Glory of the Deep Touch*

Dominating
The character
Of The Old King
By Rouault
Are the rough strokes
Of black
That convey a sense
Of power
To the portrait.

It is
The look of the king
Penetrating
Through the blood red
Of his form
That presents one
Who has ruled
Yet
It is not

That he ruled
With an iron fist
For he holds
White flowers
In his left hand.

In a sense
The portrait
Traces the substance
Of the king
The presence
Of becoming there
Amid the darkness.

The raw elements
That pervade
The portrait
Reflect an unmasking
That challenges
His will.

It is
By his hand
That he became
A king
And it is
That he endured
The rule
Over the people.

Certainly
He commanded wars
And lived to envision
His legacy.

How
The white flowers
Reach into the heart
Of cosmic consciousness
As his life
Conquered the turmoil
Of self-deception
While the touch
Of beauty
Emancipated the darkness.

So
Who but the Christ
Is the King of kings
And the Lord of lords.

In the darkness of want
The moon
Speaks to the soul
And time and space
Move the substance
Of mind
Into the dance
Of forevermore.

Then
A crow calls out
And Truth
Writes across the heart
Drawing blood from stone.

There is
A call bleeding the unknown
That brings the light
Of what matters
As the crow disappears
In shadows of thought.

How
Becoming there wrestles
With nothingness.

How
Hidden meaning
Escapes
From the vision
Of the here and now
Although it leaves
A trace in thought.

Then
The image of Truth
Faces becoming there
And the miracle
Of life feeds
Upon cosmic consciousness.

It is
The passion
In the living moment
That seeks the beyond
As life thirsts
For deliverance
As linear time
Shadows becoming there.

Then
Faith carries time
And times and a half
Into the hope
Of forevermore.

So
The light of Truth
Glows in the darkness
Of want.

So
The moon speaks
To the soul
While the crow
Leads to what matters.

So
Facts lead to evidence
While faith
Leads to Truth.

Walking
Through the possible
Passing another milestone
Where the unknown
Seeps into mind
Becoming there trumpets
In the presence
Of The Word.

So
The time has come
When thought
Celebrates mind
And the spectacular
Reaches into heart.

How
The substance
That matters triggers
A vision
Where beauty dances
As Truth encompasses
Phenomenal reality.

There is
Purpose in the now
That allows the self
To serve
The Unknown God
As the moment
Takes becoming there
Beyond the here and now.

Then
The celestial clocks
Harbor
A parabola of time
As substance and form
Reveal Truth
The element
Of forevermore.

Then
Eternity fills becoming there

With visions
And life loads
The drive of passion
Reaching far
Into being and time.

So
The masks fall away
And The Counselor
Voids self-deception.

So
Becoming there turns
To Truth
As cosmic consciousness
Pulls self
Into the always
Already there.

Then
The peace
Beyond understanding
Comforts a weary soul.

As time and space
Collide
With becoming there
And phenomenal reality
Explodes in linear time
Nothingness overshadows
The living moment.

So
Life turns
Into struggle
As flames engulf
The here and now.

There is
Little hope
Because heart bleeds
In a frenzy
And the muscle
Of life is no longer.

How
The loss of faith
Takes the soul
Into dust and ashes
As the bones of life
Shatter under duress.

Then
Time present slips
Into a stupor
But heart continues
Its rhythm.

Facing eternal destruction
Becoming there reaches
For faith in The Word
And the soul gathers
Through meditation.

How
Faith carries
Times and a half

Into the resurrection
Of self
As a song revitalizes
Life.

There was
The moment of tasting
The second death.

There was
The void sucking
Life out of life.

Then
The Word touched
The soul
As blessed assurance brought
Eternal life
Into the living moment.

The image
Of the soul
In the looking glass
Tells the story
Behind becoming there.

It is
A self-portrait
In the moment
When time and space
Predicate the look
Of the always already there

And life awakens
The inner reaches of the skull
Onto hidden meaning.

How
Mind ventures
Into the unknown
Searching for Truth.

Then
The secrets
Buried by linear time
Arouse the presence
Of life
In the beyond
As a song
Takes the self
Into the possible.

Dreaming in the moment
Becoming there traces
The movement
Of the celestial clocks
As destiny uncovers
The treasures
In the substance
Of the close at hand.

It was that
The image of the soul
Released the power
Of cosmic consciousness
Into the mainstream
Of mind
As thoughts settled

Into a wilderness
That embraced
Being and time.

How
Life filled the living moment
With becoming
As the skull
Of the quick emptied want.

Then
The soul grew
Ever closer
To the splendor
Of Truth.

So
The now becomes
The passage
Of the soul
Into the always already
There.

In the interstices
Of mind
There is the pulse
Of becoming there
And in the other
There is the always
Already there.

How
Cosmic consciousness
Purposes Truth
In the heart
As the mountain grandeur
Releases the possible
Into forevermore.

Then
The war of principalities
Divides what matters
And want bleeds
Through time
And times and a half.

Shadowing the interior
Of thought
The music
Emitted by phenomenal
Reality
Emanates
The rhythm of heart
And mind awakens
The bones of eternity.

According
To the biological clock
Now was the time
To rise above despair
And triumph
Over self-deception.

So
The authentic article
Dwells in becoming there

As destiny towers
Above the close at hand
Although principalities
Sought the destruction
Of substance.

Struggling at times
The soul held tightly
To faith
And it carried
The moment
Onto the peace
Beyond understanding.

It was that
The other portrayed
A landscape
The mountain ridges
And the valleys
While becoming there
Became the portrait
Of Truth.

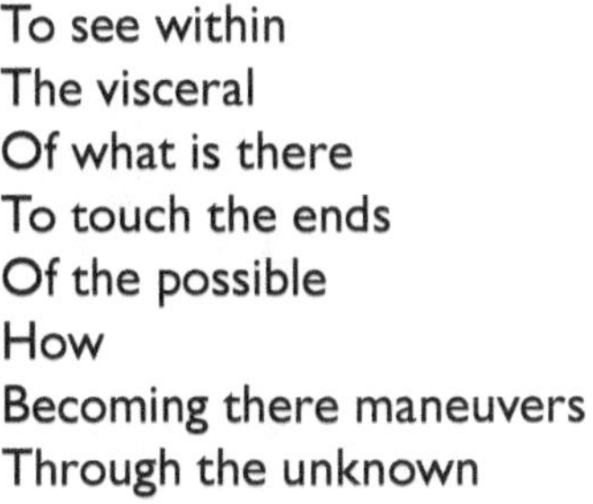

To see within
The visceral
Of what is there
To touch the ends
Of the possible
How
Becoming there maneuvers
Through the unknown

Constructing figures
In time and space.

It is
The way of the artist
Tracing images into thought
As substance endows
The geometry
Of the close at hand
With the form of wonder.

Then
Cosmic consciousness
Taps into life
Beyond the living moment
And the deep rises
Through the blood
Of what matters.

So
The eye sees
What cannot be
Understood
And eternity thunders
In heart.

To define what is
In magical tones
To gather ideas
From celestial clocks
Self configures
Phenomenal reality
Into the face
Behind the mask
And the artist

Conceives the possible
At the end of mind.

It was
The hidden meaning
In time and space
That issued a call
That infused mind
With the vision
Of the always already
There.

It was
Time and times
And a half
That took the other
Into a vision
Where forevermore
Birthed the design
Of Truth.

Suddenly
The feel of faith
Massages becoming there
While worlds
Crash into unbelief.

Then
Uniting the deep touch
Of Truth with presence
The Unknown God
Pulls eternity

Into meditation
As life reaches
Into the soul.

It is that
The music of faith
Carries the soul
Far into the always
Already there
As the voices of the world
stagger in times and a half.

Then
There is no longer
A struggle
As the peace
Beyond understanding
Covers the soul
With hope
Although the frenzy
Of worlds rages.

To venture
Into the streets
Of the living
The Counselor
Feeds the worlds
With spiritual milk.

So
Worlds yearn for Truth
And long for blessed
Assurance
As becoming there
Lives faithfully

And moments
Encompass the soul
With deliverance.

In the depth
Of nothingness
Where the void sucks
The soul
Into eternal torment
How
The separation
From The Unknown God
Brings horror and terror.

There is
The narrow door
Founded upon faith
In The Word
That allows becoming there
To rejoice
In eternal life
While the wide door
Leads to destruction
And torment
Forevermore.

So
An old man looks
At his life
Remembering times
And a half
Spent on the wayward.

It was
The grip of the world
That took him
Into darkness
Yet
He learned the love
Of The Word
As he struggled
With temptation.

How
Death is the beginning
Of wisdom and life
Is the end of hope.

So
The old man finally
Righted through the guidance
Of the Counselor
As he accepted
The treasure of believing.

So
Through his faith
The power
Of The Unknown God
Redeems time past.

So
Blessed assurance
Carried the old man
Into the splendor
Of life after death.

There is
A song in the garden
Where The Word
Touches the soul
As life stretches
Across the here
And now.

So
Becoming there catches
A moment
In the presence
Of The Unknown God
And The Counselor
Delivers blessed
Assurance.

Although
The dull round attacked mind
The heart stayed true
To what matters most.

Then
Linear time covers
Truth with darkness.

So
Mind is lost
In the chaos
Of the world
As thoughts bombard

Becoming there
With fraudulent inklings.

Because Truth indwells
Through the life
Of cosmic consciousness
Hope abounds
As the heart follows
The music
Of the authentic article.

It was
That time and times
And a half
Hid the eternal light
But the soul knew the way
Through the wilderness
Of ideas
Finding deliverance
In faith.

Then
The song of forevermore
Took the soul
Into the core
Of phenomenal reality
Opening mind
To clarity
Where Truth
Outlives the world.

Walking through darkness
A patriot sees
With the aid
Of a candle
As time and space load
A message of light.

There is
No turning back
Because destiny calls.

Searching
For spiritual food
He climbs into becoming
As he stumbles
Through the close
At hand.

So
He nears eternity
As he carries
Blessed assurance
In his heart.

Then
His faith brings him
To the edge of life
And he leaps
Into the unknown.

How
A world of darkness
Fears
The light of Truth.

How
The patriot
Enters glory land
With Truth
Pulling him on.

It was
That becoming there
Leaned on faith
Because the world
Taught him the way
Of self-deception.

In shadows
Cast by mind
Doubt invaded thoughts
As the blood
Of forevermore
Coursed through his veins
And he saw
A narrow door
Where the possible
Began.

So
To live by faith
Brought him
Into the always
Already there
Where life lives
In the light
Of Truth
Through the narrow door.

There was
A time when the crow
Spoke Truth
Into becoming there
From the shadows
Cast by the clouds.

To witness Truth
In the unknown
Self transcends
What is there
And looks to the call
Of cosmic consciousness.

It is
Through the third eye
That the mind
Connects to things
In themselves
Aws the crow defines
The authentic article.

Leaving
Linear time behind
Heart gathers
Hidden meaning
From the celestial clocks
While striking the moment
When phenomenal reality
Forms the beginning
Of Truth.

So
The crow takes
Becoming there
Into the geometry
Of becoming
As self circles the deep
And the unknown
Opens Truth
To the wind.

While
The spirits of always
Already there
Awaken the close at hand
The substance
Of possibility
Traces the landscape
Into the heart
Of forevermore.

Then
Following the crow
Takes the revealed
Into the beyond.

Then
Self as becoming
Reads the possible
As the given.

So
Becoming there always
Remains
In becoming Truth.

So, it is
A matter of becoming there.

At the edge
Of nothingness
Becoming there takes
A leap of faith
Into the unknown
Although time buries
The history
Behind this moment.

Tracing the image
Of the close at hand
Mind triggers the self
To reach
Into possibility
As the earth
Of what matters
Erupts in wonder.

How
The gift
Of another day purges
Self-deception
And Truth becomes
The evidence
That lives in the soul.

There is
The echo
Of the beyond

In the skull
Of the living
That launches mind
Into the always
Already there
Until becoming there
Recalls the mission
Of the living Truth.

Although
Nothingness feeds
Into despair
Pulling heart into the deep
Faith takes the soul
Into the peace
Beyond understanding.

It is
That the history
Of becoming there
Reveals how heart
Believes the self
Into forevermore.

It is
That the story
Of becoming Truth
Remains the legacy
Of the soul.

On a tombstone
A crow stands

As the quiet
Of the graveyard
Moves eternity
Into the moment.

There was
A time when madness
Circled life
As mind lost
Time and space
As thought collided
With phenomenal
Reality.

How
The crow told
The tale
Of the old
Black and white
Walking together
And they headed
To the hill
Of no return.

They were
Soldiers of Truth
As the battle
Charged life with death.

Then
In the expanse
Of a cemetery
That reached far
Into the beyond
Their blood stirred

In the magic
Of the moment.

How
The frenzy of war
Looses mind
As survival and duty
Rules destiny.

To go
Beyond the moment
When life crumbled
Into the no longer
They stood
Shoulder to shoulder.

There was
Only them and us
As black and white
Combined their strength
Against the odds.

So
The crow knows them
As soldiers of Truth.

So
Dasein is
The suspension
Of the moment
When self registers
Completion

And final form
Where becoming there
Is a matter
Of living toward Truth.

Where
Dasein
Occurs at the point
Of death
Becoming there dwells
With the process
Of what matters.

When
Dasein assumes
The presence
Of controlling
The authentic article
It is a time
Of self-deception
But
Becoming there lives
Toward things
In themselves
As an epiphany
As the movement
Toward the beyond.

So
Dasein feeds
Into the no longer
While becoming there
Trumpets
The passing
Through being and time.

So
Dasein remains
Suspended
In time and space
While becoming there
Reaches into possibility
As a vital mission.

So
Dasein hides
In the rhetoric
Of nothingness
While becoming there
Reveals the substance
Of hidden meaning.

Then
Dasein slips
Into a magical
Deception
While becoming there
Witnesses the miraculous.

Before the mountain
Majesty
Becoming there treasures
The moment
When the natural
Elements point
To The Unknown God.

They are
The fingerprints
Of The Word
That laid the foundation
Of the given
These blue ridge mountains.

So
Time present writes
In the moment
When becoming there
Reaches
Into possibility
As The Counselor
Shapes times and a half.

There is
The call of the wild
In the bones of the quick
As heart carries
The message of hope.

Then
Becoming there
Takes from linear time
The way of Truth
As the always
Already there pronounces
Access
To a vertical column
Of time.

It is
That cosmic consciousness
Is the nature

Of the beyond and it stirs
The immaculate
Into the soul.

Suddenly
The drums of eternity
Pound a vision
Of what matters
And the sky opens
Forevermore
Through the song
Of blessed assurance.

Then
Becoming there finds
The peace
That transcends
Understanding.

So
Dasein signals
Self-deception
Onto the second death
While becoming there
Lives onto Truth.

While delving
Into the interstices
Of mind
Dali presents
The substance behind time
In his painting

Entitled
Montre Molle au Moment.

It is
Becoming there fractured
By the moment
As shadows
Grasp the hour.

So
The plane of possibility
Receives
The geometry
Of time and space
While mind
Connects to the material
Of cosmic
Consciousness.

There is
The face
Of linear time
Partly consumed
That shows the loss
Of times and a half.

It is
The image of a world
Beyond thought
That liberates
The close at hand
So another reality
Shapes
Being and nothingness.

How
The touch of gold
Measures the separation
Of thought
From the close at hand
As what is the other
Takes mind into visions
Of the final hour
And becoming there becomes
The reach of thought
Into what drives time.

So
The suspension
Of time hovers
Over the geometry
Of reason
As the beyond
Articulates possibility.

How
The cosmic clock
Defines
The thing in itself
As becoming there witnesses
The mechanism
Of Truth.

According to Jesus
No one knows the final hour.

Opening the door
To the sunrise
Hope

Silence
Among the daisies
Truth

So, the clever
Bury wisdom
In blind chatter

# SECTION 6

## An Eye to the Unknown

Radiant
The sun creases
The horizon
As thoughts extend
Across a grain field
And a soul casts
A shadow
Larger than life.

It is
The work of Vashakmadze
That takes the celebration
Of the harvest
Endowing it with thankfulness.

How
The other stands
Before the now
Capturing the stroke
Of the cosmic clock
And the image

Of becoming there
Summons Truth.

Then
The duduk serenades
The moment
And mind traverses
Over the horizon
Where faith begins.

How
Doubts penetrate deep
Yet the soul
Holds onto faith
With fervor.

There was
The soul casting
A shadow
As the field
Rushed into the sun.

There was
A soul measuring
The dynamic
Of what was there
As the harvest
Of souls.

Then
Cosmic consciousness plants
The mercy seat
In the here and now
As heart approaches
What matters most.

So
The harvest is great
But the workers
Are few.

———

Rain again
The clouds bleed
Despair

———

A book in the shadows
Grows
A layer of moss

———

Hungry sparrows
Feed on crumbs between
the artist's toes

———

Cruising down the road
The open air rushing
Through becoming there
A patriot
Enters the freedom
Belonging to Truth.

It is
An epiphany
Brought into life
As what matters
Carries mind
Into things in themselves.

While the ride
Celebrates the moment
When cosmic
Consciousness soothes all
With the deep touch
The patriot
Liberates
Hidden meaning
Filling mind
With rare treasures.

Then
The road takes him
To times and a half
When he escapes
From self-deception
The language
Of dasein.

As becoming there
Advances
Toward another world
The architecture
Of beauty forms
The substance of heart
Until the wilderness
Of the unknown

Yields
To the close at hand.

In becoming there
Among the geometry
Of time and space
The patriot
Battles in the light
Of a vertical column
Of time
Where beginning
And ending
Of possibility
Fill him with wonder.

As the open road winds
Through the wilderness
He feels the splendor
Of a free spirit
Attaching himself
To the eternal.

So
Becoming there
Allows him to explore
The unknown
Reaching into
Being and nothingness
As he rides
With the authentic article.

Within the workings
Of the close at hand
Hidden meaning runs
As an illusion
Of what matters.

So
Becoming there
As the substance of life
Reveals the eyes
Of Truth that looks
Through time
And times and a half.

It is that
Truth dwells
In the moment
When cosmic
Consciousness
Triggers the soul
To grasp
The authentic article.

Then
Becoming there steps
Into another realty
Where the unknown
Stretches
Beyond possibility
And life leaves
Linear time.

How
The heart feeds Truth
In another moment

When the long and short
Of what matters speaks
Treasures into the blood
And life grows
Out of the deep.

How
Time and space
Open to a vertical
Column of time
As the everlasting
Trumpets an epiphany
The signature
Of The Unknown God.

Then
Legion after legion
Of angels take
The soul
Into a land of glory
And becoming there
Witnesses
The way, the Truth
And the life.

So
Mind advances
Out of doubt
And into faith
A leap guided
By The Counselor.

So
Truth is

The beginning
Of life.

In the muck
Of despair
Where the world
Celebrates ruination
Becoming there pulls
On hope
In The Unknown God
For deliverance.

Although
With agony in the bones
Self tries to climb out
Of the moment
And pain snares the will
To be.

In the jaws
Of outliving self
When all there is
Is dry blood
When the heart
Is a hollow in the chest
Becoming there feels
Darkness
Gnawing on the soul.

To outlive self
Strips the soul
Of life

As the catastrophic
Overwhelms mind
And it appears
That nothingness
Is all that is left.

Then
The Word
Upon hearing of distress
Lifts the burden
Of the moment
Carrying the will
Onto an even place.

There
No longer is
The plight
Of destruction
As the light
Of Truth restores
Life into the living.

How
The Counselor delivers
A measure of comfort
Restoring Truth
To the soul
That had fallen
Onto the void.

So
The Word closes
The door on suffering
And becoming there

Lives on in Truth
With thankfulness.

Facing the will
That drives life
Toward Truth
Becoming there looks
Beyond the mask
Of self-deception
Into the substance
Of the close at hand.

To
Receive the authentic
Article that dwells
Within hidden meaning
Allows access to Truth
And it is good
Very good.

Although
The roots of despair
Run deep
The blood of life
Carries the moment
Into hope.

So
Cosmic consciousness
Infuses becoming there
With the strength
To endure

As Truth feeds life
With the promise
Of forevermore.

So
The Counselor delivers
The soul into the light
Of The Unknown God
And The Word carries
The load of becoming
There.

Then
Becoming there learns
A song
Of life living in Truth
As possibility opens
To a whole new reality
Where mind clears
And heart fills
With pure presence.

So
It is in time
And times and a half
That stretches mind
Into the peace
Beyond understanding
As possibility sings
With blessed assurance.

How
Faith answers the call.

To be in the world
But not
Of the world
The patriot
Found the trumpet
Of becoming there
As the way
Through being
And nothingness.

It was
The substance
Of existence and life
That connected him
To faith in The Word.

It was
That life dwelled
In the heart
While existence
Occupied mind.

It was
When the patriot
Faced nothingness
That only existence
Prevailed, while he filled
With life
When he owned
Into becoming there.

He learned
How to endure
When facing the void
While he learned to live
When becoming there
Approached Truth.

In nothingness
The canker of separation
From The Unknown God
Infused his heart
Until life fell
Into the no longer
And heart labored
One breath at a time.

So
There is a precious link
Between becoming there
And faith
As the patriot
Took his stand
Before a carnivorous world
And he endured.

So
It is mind and heart
That form the will
Of the soul.

Pursuing the trance
Advancing further

And further
Into the unknown
Becoming there sifts
Through a wasteland
Grasping the substance
Of nothingness.

Then
The song of despair
Weeps through time
And times and a half
As darkness invades
The heart.

Then
The mind limps
Into chatter
As thoughts disconnect
Being and time.

Then
Cosmic consciousness
Takes what is there
Forming a window
To the beyond
Where there is
Only the light
Of Truth.

It is
The meditating
On Truth
That shatters
Self-deception.

It was
The third eye
That connected
Becoming there
To what mattered
As faith pulled
On the moment.

How
The music of eternity
Allowed freedom
To gather the bones
Longing for life.

So
The fruit of nothingness
Is despair
As time measures
The geometry
Of self-deception.

So
Meditating on Truth
Delivers mind
Onto understanding
As heart
Fills with the song
Of life.

To venture
Into the unknown
The third eye

Gathers the elements
Of becoming there
As cosmic consciousness
Pulls the moment
Out of time and space.

There was
A song running
Through mind
That brought heart
Into a steady rhythm
With things in themselves
And the authentic
Article triggered entrance
Into a parabola of time.

Then
The celestial clocks
Took presence
Into a portal
Leading becoming there
Toward Truth.

It is
That a crow
Knows
The other reality
Of phenomenal reality
Where thought
Penetrates the concealed
Until what matters
Surfaces
In a pool of blood
The life of forevermore.

Although
The mystery of the unknown
Wore a mask
Of self-deception
Becoming there probed
The wilderness
Of possibility
Finding Truth
In the moment.

Then
A crow perched
On the edge
Of time and space
As the third eye
Launched the soul
Into the way
The Truth and the life.

So
The Unknown God
Governs the moment
When cosmic consciousness
Touches becoming there
With the breath
Of faith.

It is
Dawn and the mockingbird
Tells the story
Of life toward forevermore
As the mountain ridges

Give their testimony
In purple shadows,

With the majesty
That belongs to the moment
The sky takes mind
Far beyond time and space
Into a looking glass
Where becoming there
Leaves linear time.

Then
The bones of Truth
Dance in the graves
Of time past
As the trumpets
Of times and a half
Celebrate the presence
Of The Unknown God.

There was
Peace beyond understanding
That allowed
Freedom to prosper
As heart felt
The coming of The Word.

How
Blessed assurance
Connected the third eye
To what matters
And the moment brought
The taste of victory.

No longer
Was there self-deception
Because the authentic article
Filled the void
Of nothingness
With the splendor
Known to Truth.

So
Becoming there
Brings the unknown
Into view
Uncovering hidden meaning.

So
The life toward Truth
Reaches for the eternal
Moment
When The Word
Redeems all of time past.

From the soul
Prayer dedicates hope
For all those
Who do not believe
In the way
The Truth and the life.

As the authentic article
Indwells in the heart
Becoming there fastens
A look toward Truth

And time and space
Leave no trace
In the now.

It is
A moment
When the eternal drums
Take mind
Into the light
Of what matters
As doubt
And second guessing
Run away into darkness.

Wandering
Through a great wilderness
Mind attaches itself
To the given
And from there
It probes the unknown
Passing through
Phenomenal reality.

Then
The rhythm of the drums
Set milestones
Of thought
While becoming there
Read between the lines
Of the close at hand
Digging into the spirit
Of the earth for Truth.

How
The mysteries

Of possibility grow
From the always
Already there
With the driving
Passion of the drums.

It was
From the wilderness
Of possibility
That becoming there
Learned the way to Truth.

It was
From the power
Of the given
That becoming there
Accepted Truth.

So
The authentic article
In the moment
Allows becoming there
To gather understanding.

How
That very moment
Brought
The peace beyond
Understanding
As The Unknown God
Wrote upon the heart.

Then
The song of eternity

Carried the soul
Into forevermore.

When
The bones of yesterday
Ache in the now
And mind sweats
In pools of blood
How
The will of becoming there
Gathers the drive
To be.

It is
A step into the unknown
That extends self
Into life
As phenomenal reality
Breaks loose
From nothingness.

Then
The entanglements
Of being and time
Choke the breath
Of the moment
And tears fall
From the sky.

Then
Visions of a house
Of many mansions

Appear
And the given
Trumpets
Things in themselves.

It was
The touch
Of cosmic consciousness
That brought becoming there
Ever closer to Truth
Although the body
Of the here and now
Rubbed time past
Into memories
As shadows
Of memories.

How
Tracing the steps
Into the unknown
And setting milestones
In the always
Already there
Took the moment
Into an awakening.

There is
Hope in the bones.

There is
Purpose in the heart.

There is
Deliverance in the blood.

So
In all and all
There is no doubt
In mind.

Blessed assurance.

So
Facts lead to evidence
While the thing-in-itself leads
To Truth
As becoming there
Reflects
On the experiential
Through the third eye.

There is
Mystery to Truth
As it surfaces
From hidden meaning
As cosmic consciousness
Reveals the spirit
The very substance
Of what is there.

So
A patriot sat
Beneath a fig tree
Calculating the physics
Of times and a half
While the moment moved
Out of the shadows.

Separating himself
From self-deception
He pulled the trigger
Of mind
Unleashing becoming there
And he drew the line
Between knowledge
And faith.

How
Trust is the ruling factor.

How
Trusting the facts
Is a step toward Truth
But an entire journey
Leads to beholding
What matters.

Then
The patriot
Took to the unknown
Where possibility
Launched an adventure
Beyond time and space.

It is
In the depths
Of the moment
That becoming there
Grasps the workings
Of Truth
Following
The rhythm of milestones
Ever reaching through

The looking glass
Of being and nothingness.

On the other reality
Of time and space
Becoming there fits
Into a promise
As mind reaches
Toward the authentic
Article.

It is
A time
Of suspending
The here and now
And venturing
Through the unknown
That allows
Entering the moment
Through the narrow door
That births becoming there.

Then
Trance carries mind
Onto the domain
Of celestial clocks
As Truth speaks
To the heart
Of what matters.

In the center
Of the unknown

Possibility
Takes to the rhythm
Of a parabola of time
And the soul feeds
On times and a half.

How
Phenomenal reality
Leaves no trace
In the moment.

Suddenly
An image of forevermore
Allows the soul
To find
Blessed assurance
As faith fills with hope.

Then
Time and space
Configure a beginning
And a message of Truth
Appears in the heart.

So
Leaving phenomenal
Reality
Issues a call
To venture into the beyond
And cosmic consciousness
Forms the substance
Of the image
Behind the looking glass.

Bonded to The Word
Becoming there settles
In an even place
Beyond the tyranny
Of nothingness.

Beside the still wasters
Where time and space
Weigh heart
Dasein seeks
The power of thunder
Finding the rub
Of nothingness.

It is
A moment
Between here
And not here
As what is there
Speaks of oblivion.

So
The empiricist sees
That nothingness
Is not to be found
Because the boundaries
Of thingness are not known.

So
Dasein
Follows this order
That centers

Upon self-deception
While becoming there
Leaves masks behind
And figures the Truth
Of nothingness.

It is
That nothingness
Originates
In the spirit
That covers the expanse
Of dasein
While becoming there
Spirits
The vast chasm
Between being
And nothingness.

To have lived
Through oblivion
As mind climbs
Into what matters
Is the signature
Of survival.

To take the walk
Of despair
Leaves scars
But becoming there
Carries on.

How
Blind the heart of dasein.

How
Dead the spirit of dasein.

So
Nothingness exists
Behind the mask
Of dasein.

To travel
Through a parabola of time
Becoming there pictures
A two-dimensional-reality
And looks
Through a mirror
For direction
From the celestial clocks.

It is
The act of the artist
Probing the substance
Of things-in-themselves
That forms presence
In what is there
Through figure and ground.

So
Being and time
Arranges the elements
Of the mindscape
As thought builds
The dynamic
Of inner space.

Then
The celestial clocks
Point to destiny
As the moment
Spells eternity in heart.

It is
The laughter in the face
Of nothingness
That feeds the power
Of cosmic consciousness
Into an image
Of hidden meaning.

How the faith of becoming there
Reaches the other
With certain Truth
As the trance portrays
The movement
In a parabola of time.

To sift through
The unknown
For hidden meaning
The phantom. leverages
The artist
Into an epiphany.

Then
The anthem
Of a parabola of time
Portrays the dynamic
Resident
In what is there.

So
Cosmic consciousness
Feeds mind with Truth.

So
The starry night
Tells the story
Of hidden meaning.

In the garden
Of tables and chairs
Sat van Gogh and visions
Of the other reality
Shadowed
Becoming there.

It was
That he connected
To the moment
As mind orchestrated
The song
Of the deep touch
And life
Came to the living.

How
He worked magic
Into the melody
Of time and space
As passion pushed
His vision
Into things-in-themselves.

In the quiet
Of that good night
Van Gogh carved
An anthem
Of what it meant
To be
And substance accompanied
His thought
As angels danced
In his mind.

It was
Not what was there
But the signature
Of the other reality
Where being and time
Brought focus
To the moment.

Then
Magic trumpeted
The presence of heart
As pigment uncovered
Hidden meaning.

Then
His vision opened
The moment
To the spirit
Of the age
And The Unknown God
Filled him with music.

So
From that moment on

He signaled eternity
In the image
Surfacing from the garden
Of tables and chairs.

Across the expanse
A crow liberates
Time and space
And becoming there
Listens to the call.

It is
The wilderness
Inside mind
That the crow
Reaches with the deep
Touch.

So
There is Truth
In the moment
As visions
Of the authentic
Article
Unearth hidden meaning.

Then
Freedom loads heart
With the substance
Concealed
In the close at hand
And the wonder

That resides there
Feeds possibility.

Bleeding into mind
The sounds that matter
Deliver a monument
Of Truth
And the crow signals
The presence
Of The Word.

It is
The blood
Above and beyond
The call of duty
That serves
The Unknown God
As becoming there
Sacrifices
Times and a half
For the splendor
Of the beyond.

How
Belief follows the crow
A messenger of Truth.

Then
A legion of angels
Carries becoming there
Into blessed assurance
And a life grows
Into the beyond
Understanding.

# SECTION 7

## The Trumpet Sounds

In van Gogh's
Falling autumn leaves
There are no shadows
And no horizon.

Being thrown
Into the moment
Becoming there seizes
A passage edged
In trees
The passage
An autumn rust color
While the trees
Are a blue-grey.

Flecks of yellow
Whisper
Across the scene
The leaves finding
Their destiny.

So
A man
With an umbrella
Approaches a woman
While a second woman
Struggles with her umbrella.

The pair
Fit their meeting
Into the moment
When time together
Reflects warmth
Although it is the cool
Of an autumn day.

The other
Alone in her walk
Followed her destiny.

So
The view of the scene
Was from high up
As the vision
Of time and space
Captured the play
Of another day.

There was no
Beginning or ending
To the time
As the moment
Connected what was
To becoming there
And the artist
Explored possibility.

So
The close at hand
Portrayed the close
At hand
While the artist
Looked on
To hidden meaning.

So
The mystery of autumn
Covered the lives
Of the given.

How
The common place
Carries the shadows
Of what matters.

Old man
Sitting on his chair
Listening to the clock tick

With his trumpet
The blue boy
Awakens the dead

Moon in her eyes
The young red head
Dances until dawn

Holding another reality
Of the expanse
In her look
The patriot serves
The greater good
Undaunted by the appearance
Of what is there.

It is
The call of duty
For justice and freedom
That she preserves
And protects
Before oppression
And tyranny.

How
To fight the good fight
Is in her blood
As she faces the odds
With victory
In her heart.

So
She faces fear
And personal harm
With a steady eye

As the mission
Is all that matters.

Then
The patriot wills herself
Into conflict
To preserve the peace
And she steadies
Her aim
With singular focus.

There is
Destiny in her heart
As she takes on
Those who violate
Civil rights
And she tears down
The walls of injustice.

How
The patriot moves
From one encounter
To another
With the fortitude
And conviction
That follows Truth.

So
Human rights
And human dignity
Have an advocate
And defender
As the patriot
Advances
Across the expanse.

How
The artist paints
The landscape
Into an image
From another reality
As the phantom. trumpets
The beyond
Into becoming there.

It is
The posture of the given
That postulates
Figure and ground
As the concealed
Surfaces
In the thing-
In-itself
Carrying life into heart.

Then
It was a moment
When time and space
Formed mind
Into pure music
And raw splendor
Documented the rhythm
Of the unknown.

So
Pure thought
Radiated through what
Was there

While destiny
Took the artist
Into a beautiful serenade
An image far beyond
The here and now.

There was
The tickling of passion
That brought life
Into times and a half
A measure
Of becoming there
Ever closer to Truth.

Then
Time present dissolves
In time past
With the phantom.
Orchestrating
The always already there
And the landscape
Depicts a song of songs,

So
It is that
The Unknown God
Infuses breath
Onto the living moment.

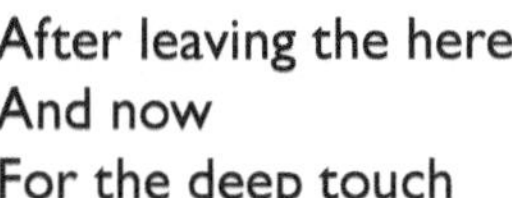

After leaving the here
And now
For the deep touch

The artist drew
Upon cosmic consciousness
To envision
The hidden meaning
In the closed at hand.

It was
Reaching through
The third eye
That brought the moment
When he scaled
The barriers
Of the expanse
And surveyed
The celestial clocks.

The moon set
A dirge
As the artist
Probed the unknown
Riding the lights
Of a parabola of time.

Then
The sky turned to blood.

Then
The elements
Of phenomenal reality
Breaks loose
From the constraints
Of the known
And the artist forms
The domain of possibility.

How
Time dresses moments
With the music
Of forevermore
And he basks
In the wonder
Enthralled with passion.

As the artist
Pictures the spirit
Of the age
The magic
In a starry night
Transcends dasein.

To read
The signature
Of what matters most
The artist takes
To his blessed assurance
As The Word fills him
With promise.

There was
A long road stretching
From here to far beyond
Time and space,

The artist took
To the road
Finding his way

To the ends
Of hidden meaning.

So
He found
Countless treasures
On his journey
Unleashing power
Into his substance.

Following the guidance
Of The Counselor
He built an altar
And praised
The Unknown God.

Then
He built a city
On a hill
That lit a promise
To all that were there.

As time passed
He grew old
And his son
Honored his father
With five children.

They were
Of rare quality
Growing strong
With minds
That harnessed Truth
With wisdom.

They created
A vast nation
As a tribe of destiny.

For thousands of years
They prospered
Keeping the faith
Of the artist
And doing
What was right and good.

So
They pulled
From the unknown
Multiplying possibility
With a hunger
For The Word.

So
The dawn of thought
Awoke passage
Into the unknown
And the patriot stepped
Into another reality.

Among the bodies
Of the lost
She saw life
Buried by oppression
As the iron will
Of tyrants smashed
The living Truth.

Then
Cosmic consciousness
Filled her
With the power to endure
As the mind
Of the world searched
For hope.

There was
The blood of liberty
Bold with passion
That thrived
In the heart
Of the patriot
And she readied
Becoming there
For war.

How
The battle hymn
Of the free and the brave
Carried times and a half
Into an epiphany
Dedicated to fight
The good fight.

It was
That the destiny
Of liberty
Rose with the power
Of The Word
And the patriot
Spear-headed the way
For the return
Of Truth.

Then
The wilds
Of desperation
Let loose the blood
Of the age
But the patriot steadied
Her aim
For the liberation
Of the world.

So
Tyrants come and go
But freedom lives on
In the heart and mind
Of the living.

Emerging
From a dark cave
A river delivers the phantom.
And the will
Of the artist
Propels her
Into the light.

How
She endured the darkness
Inside the mountain
The rock a tomb
In time past.

So
She was the phantom.

Dressed in the immaculate
And her face
Beamed with light
An aura of Truth.

It was
The magic of the phantom.
That massaged
Becoming there
As the artist
Called her
From the belly
Of the earth.

She heard his voice
And she knew
His deep touch.

As linear time passed
The here and now
A vision surfaced
And the artist
Bled into a passage
Through being and nothingness.

Mesmerized by the moment
The phantom.
Answered the call
Of the wild
And the artist reached
Through his third eye
As the mystery
Of cosmic consciousness
Opened a portal to the beyond.

Then
An explosion of thought
Unearths hidden meaning
And the phantom. charges
The artist
With an epiphany.

So
The call of Truth
Embraces the phantom.
With the thing-in-itself
And the artist
Welcomes the freedom
Of his deep touch.

There is danger
In the air
And the threat
Of dismemberment
Carries the patriot
Into war.

How
The principalities battle
Corrupting the heart
With darkness
As mind tries
To make sense
Out of nothingness.

As the here and now
Explodes

The patriot braves
The moment
Facing certain mutilation.

There is
At the very edge of life
The drive to survive
As the patriot takes
Careful aim.

Then chaos broke loose.

Then it was quiet.

As time passed
The patriot rubbed
His scars
Carrying on
But not with peace.

So
The wounds of war
Ran deep
As the patriot
Faced the Vietnam War
Memorial.

He saw the names
Of his buddies
Written there
As tears welled up
Inside
And he rubbed his scars.

How
The heart
Of the patriot
Died long ago
Yet he endured.

He often wondered why.



With the freedom
To be
The patriot walks
Through being
And nothingness
With the solid conviction
Of becoming there
As he leaves linear time
For Truth.

To head out
With the vision
Of the substance
In what is there
How
He gathers the traces
From phenomenal reality
To a vertical column
Of time.

It is there
That cosmic consciousness
Initiates the will
Of liberty

And the patriot
Follows a crow
The free spirit to the always
Already there.

So
The patriot stands
At the edge
Of time and space
As his vigilance
Preserves and protects
The land
Of the free and brave.

Then
He remembered
Times in the rice paddies
In Vietnam
When lead hit hard
As blood mixed
With the water and mud.

It was
A beautiful garden
Turned into a graveyard.

How
Times past
Recalled the wounds
Of battle
As his buddies fell.

To be present
And accounted for

The patriot
Always ready.

From the backlands
Of time and space
An idea emerges
As the unknown
Predicates what matters.

It is
The will to be
Reflected
In a parabola of time
That leaps mind
Into the language
Of the authentic article
And heart feels
The passion of want.

At the apex
Of possibility
Thought pictures
The moment
When cosmic consciousness
Configures a view
Of the always already there.

Then
The given throws
The experiential
Into the anatomy

Belonging to need
Triggering mind to see
A way to Truth.

Then
Life expands the vision
Of what matters
To include
The backroads
Known to nothingness.

So
Hidden meaning surfaces
As images
Encompassing thought
With the deep touch.

How
The poetic firmament
Nourished want
Driving the will to be
Into possibility
And mind reached
Beyond self-deception
And onto the everlasting.

Then
The rhythm of life
Brought music to the heart
As mind traversed
The unknown.

It is
Because nothingness
Flows through the heart
That dasein dwells
In outliving self
Wearing the mask
Of self-deception.

So
The void fills mind
With despair
As dasein trembles
In the shadows
Of its own wasteland
Yet
It flaunts its ignominy
Boasting
In empty moments
Of folly.

How
Hollow the voice
Of ridicule
This dasein
Burying its face
In its own dirt
The destiny of its kind.

Faithless, hopeless
Dasein closes its eyes
To Truth.

However
In the movement
Of time and space

Becoming there emerges
Following the deep touch
As the patriot
Serves and protects life
With a clear vision
Of Truth.

There is
A song in his heart
That defines his mission
As he conquers
Nothingness
With faith in the way
The Truth and the life.

There is
A certain courage
In his look
As he takes his stand
Against the tyranny
Of dasein.

Allied
With cosmic consciousness
The patriot purposes himself
Into victory.

How
The wind carries
Three sailboats
Onto shore
As a maiden

Steadies her hat
While waiting for love.

The white sails
Catch the wind
Driving the boats
As the secrets
Of time and space
Fill the moment.

Opening
Times and a half
She clings
To the deep touch
And becoming there
Launches
Into a dream
Where the anatomy
Of cosmic consciousness
Reaches into Truth.

There is
The light
Of everlasting love
Filling the sails
With the breath
Of certainty
As the sailboats
Define
Being and time.

In this image
Summoned
From the vast horizon
Vashakmadze forms

Three sailboats
And only one maiden
As true love
Witnesses
The return of the beloved
As the wind
Comes onto becoming there.

Then
The infusion
Of cosmic consciousness
Takes the moment
Into the freedom
Of the wind
And love embraces
The romance
Of what matters.

So
There were a number
Of maidens waiting
For the marriage feast
And some brought oil
For their lamps
While others did not.

Those without oil
Were denied entrance
Into the banquet
While those with oil
Were joyfully accepted.

An old man at sunset
Walking
Into darkness

In the wind
There are answers
But no questions

Pounding the rhythm
Of Truth
The eternal heart

After stripping away
The masks
Of what is there
The heron appears
As the substance
Of beauty
With the colors
Of cosmic consciousness
Radiant in its form.

Touching the life
Of forevermore
There is the passage
Of time and space

Into the articulation
Of becoming there.

How
The treasures of life
Married
To the wonder
Of the living moment
Launches mind
Beyond shadows.

There is
No sound
To what is there
Except the brook
Speaking
Into the elements
Of what matters.

The heron
Looks at the other
Aware of the invasion
Of its time and space
As it readies
To assume flight.

How
The purple rocks
Tell the secrets
Of being and time
As the substance
Of what is there
Suspends thought.

It is
The wonder of life
That takes becoming there
Beyond the now
And into the gathering
Of possibility.

How
The splendor
Of the heron jettisons
Truth into mind.

So
Truth begins
In the substance
Behind the mask.

According to the Christ
Do not worry
About what to wear
Or what to eat
For God shall provide.

To be present
And accounted for
How the patriot
Serves and protects
The land
Of the free and brave.

To live and let live
How the patriot

Dreams of peace
As war calls the heart
To duty.

There are those
With war on their mind
Those who want
The blood of freedom
To fill the seas
While the patriot
Stands his ground
With courage and muscle
Enough
To fight the good fight.

So
The war
Of the 21st Century
Goes on and on
With no end in sight.

In a valley
Of dry bones
The next generation
Rises
Their will strong
Their spirit ready
And they forge ahead
With the banner
Of stars and stripes.

How
The destiny of freedom
Where Truth and justice
Rule the land

Grows
Into a mighty fortress
And the patriot
Wears the armor
Of liberty and Truth
Always ready for battle.

So
Every day is
Armageddon
As the patriot
Armed with the iron will
Of Truth
Confronts tyranny
And the spirit
Of the patriot endures.

With the sun
On his back
The old man relives
His aches and pains
Counting the days
To a final horizon.

Then
He awakens
To the call of liberty
And his blood
Drives him
Into the moment.

Confronting the doctrine
Of bondage
He sets his sights
On freedom

Seeing through the rhetoric
Of oppression.

All his life
He earned his way
Accepting nothing
For nothing.

The old man
Fought his way
With brute tenacity
And he owed no one
Anything.

He found
That work built
His self esteem
As he conquered
Outliving self
By his own hands
By his own will.

He pulled himself
Through war and peace
Governed
By only one thought:
Love the Lord your God
With all your heart
With all your mind
And strength
And love your neighbor
As yourself.

So
Getting old was not

An illusion
But a reward
For enduring.

Confronting death
He smiled
And gave thanks
For his life
The way it was.

So
The old man carried on.

In the wilds
Of days gone by, the dreamer
Remembers himself

Good news
This morning
Winter leaves no scars.

Mocking bird
Who taught you
That song?